FATE Pres

Slips in Time
and Space

FATE Presents

SLIPS IN TIME AND SPACE

Compiled & Edited by
Rosemary Ellen Guiley

Visionary Living Publishing/Visionary Living, Inc.
New Milford, Connecticut

FATE Presents: Slips in Time and Space

Compiled and edited by Rosemary Ellen Guiley

Copyright 2019 by Visionary Living, Inc.

Front cover design by April Slaughter
Back cover and interior design by Leslie McAllister

ISBN: 978-1-942157-44-1 (pbk)
ISBN: 978-1-942157-45-8 (epub)

Visionary Living Publishing/Visionary Living, Inc.
New Milford, Connecticut
www.visionarylivingpublishing.com

TABLE OF CONTENTS

INTRODUCTION

One of the most disturbing mysteries is the nature of time. Is it fixed and rigid, flowing in a linear fashion from past to present to future? Or is it fluid and malleable, a moving target in a quantum sea of probabilities?

In our consensus reality, time is linear. We never live in anything but the present, but we have a past that seems immutable and a future that is uncertain. Yet, we have ample evidence that people do step out of linear time. Spontaneous, unexpected events happen when the doors of time open and individuals suddenly find themselves in a landscape that belongs to another era. These are not experiences of retrocognition, a psychic seeing into the past, or precognition, a psychic seeing into the future, but actual transports in temporary displacements of time. Call them time slips, time warps or other terms – they are bewildering at the least and terrifying at the most.

Those who return have stories to tell. But are there those who don't return? It appears it is possible to become lost in time.

We have grappled with the mystery of time for millennia. Despite our living in linear time, which constantly moves forward and not backward, our ancient myths and folklore deal with quirks and irregularities in time. In the Hindu epic, the *Mahabharata,* written about 400 BCE, there lived a king, Kakudmi, who ruled an advanced underwater domain. He was convinced that there were no men worthy enough to marry his daughter, and so he took her to Brahmaloka, the home of Brahma, to ask the god's advice. They had to wait to see Brahma, and when they were finally admitted to an audience, they were astonished to learn that everyone they had left behind in their kingdom was dead. They were in another stream of time. Brahma explained that time passes differently in different planes of existence. It all turned out well for the daughter, for Brahma joined her to Krishna's twin brother.

Similarly, according to Celtic fairy lore, time passes slowly in the fairy realm, a world of perpetual twilight. Humans who unfortunately venture down a fairy mound usually become trapped and never return. The few who do return find that many years have passed in the mortal realm, while only a few days passed in the fairy realm.

In mystical traditions, linear time does not exist, but all things happen in an ever-present now. In contrast, Isaac Newton, born in the late Renaissance, proclaimed time to be absolute. Several centuries went by before Albert Einstein arrived at the same conclusion as the mystics in that the past, present, and future all exist simultaneously, and time is relative rather than absolute. For example, people traveling in a space ship at the speed of light would age much more slowly than people on Earth. Einstein also posited that the higher a person lives above sea level, the faster he will age – potentially bad news for those who like the mountains!

Regardless of the relativity or reality of time, we need linear time in order to have a world with meaning. In Greek mythology, time itself is personified by the god Chronos, an old, stooped and gray-bearded man who governs events and makes sure that they happen one after another in linear fashion, for otherwise life would be a jumble of confusing events. How could we organize ourselves without time keeping? Disturbances in the fabric of time are deeply unsettling, and such themes have been well explored in science fiction and on shows such as Rod Serling's ground-breaking *The Twilight Zone* and Gene Roddenberry's *Star Trek*.

We have explored the idea of intentional travel through time, sometimes with the idea of changing circumstances to avoid an undesirable event. Is it possible to do so, or would we alter events so that the world we left no longer exists?

Storytellers and scientists have pondered the mechanics of time travel. Would it require a vehicle, such as the one built by the anonymous Time Traveller in H.G. Wells' 1895 classic, *The Time Machine,* or the modified DeLorean car in the 1985 hit film *Back to the Future*? Would it require the intervention of a supernatural entity such as an angel or the ghosts of Christmases in Charles Dickens' 1843 novel, *A Christmas Carol*? Or could we simply will ourselves to travel?

In the real accounts recorded throughout history, the time-space displacement happens spontaneously. For example, in 12th-century England, the villagers in tiny Woolpit, Suffolk, were shocked to find two bewildered and frightened children, a boy and a girl, in one of their wolf trap pits. They were green-skinned and could not speak any known language. The villagers did not know from whence they came, or what to do with them. Offered food, the children ate only beans. Soon the boy sickened and died, but the girl survived and learned English.

She said she and the boy came from a land lit by a perpetual light like sunset. They were out tending their flocks when they encountered a cavern and heard the sound of bells. They followed the sounds and came out the mouth of the cavern. They were immediately struck senseless by the brilliant and intense light of earthly sun, and the heavy temperature of the air. They lay unable to move for a long time and could not flee when the people arrived.

The villagers were never able to find the mysterious cavern or opening that linked their world, the Land Above, to the world of the Green Children, the Land Below.

In local interpretation, the children were regarded as fairies. They had somehow gotten transported from the fairy realm below the surface of the earth. Since time moves differently in the fairy realm, we can posit that the children were teleported through time and space. Their portal was the mysterious cavern. One can only wonder what the fairies they left behind thought of their mysterious disappearance.

It is interesting to note that following World War II, there was an explosion of reported cases of time travel and teleportation, along with reports of UFOs and a spiked interested in the paranormal. How do we account for this? Some believe the dropping of the atom bombs on Japan in 1945 ripped a hole in the Earth's space-time continuum, through which UFOs, ghosts, cryptids, mysterious entities, aliens, spirits of all kinds and doorways to parallel worlds now pour into our reality, for better or worse. They may be right.

Some of the increase in cases may be accounted for by the proliferation of media reports, which encourages more reports. FATE certainly played a role in that from its launch in 1948.

I do not think, however, that we can lay it all at the feet of the media. Other factors have changed our reality, not just the Japan bombs. Nuclear bomb testing has gone on around the world since then. In 2017, North Korea detonated a hydrogen bomb, causing a 6.3-magnitude earthquake and possibly a cave-in at the test site. The Earth has a physical integrity and a sophisticated web of energy frequencies.

Shattering the planet with bomb detonations surely has fractured pieces of the web. In addition, we have made advances in technology that bend – or have the potential to bend – the space-time fabric. Most significant is the Large Hadron Collider that went into operation in Switzerland in September 2008.

One thing is evident: we cannot close these mysterious changes/openings in space-time; they have already altered our reality. Yet, we are still governed by linear time and can only move forward – and hope we will avoid some time-space catastrophe.

Meanwhile, our personal experiences, such as those described in this book, are contributing to change as well, a piece-by-piece adding to the collective that will shift things significantly when some critical mass factor is reached. The space-time reality of our descendants is likely to be vastly different than the one we live in today.

Slips in Time and Space explores the many mysteries of time. It is divided into six sections:

Time Slips features experiences of spontaneous time relocation. Prominent psychical and paranormal researchers examine various explanations. Only one explanation fits: the people involved experienced an aberration of time. In "Bumps on the Track of Time," Brad Steiger discusses the idea that some ghost encounters actually may be time slip experiences. The "ghost" is just as startled as we are.

Years ago, I visited the Winterthur estate near Wilmington, Delaware, the former home of Henry Francis du Pont. I took a tour of the mansion and, as I always do on tour, asked the guide about ghosts. She told me an interesting story that had happened to a staff member who was closing up for the night. She was alone in this particular area. When she exited one of the rooms, she was surprised to see two figures, a man and a woman, standing in the hallway having an animated but silent conversation. They were dressed in period clothing that looked to be from the mid-20th century. As she stared at them in amazement, they turned and looked at her, and both reacted in fright. They dashed into a nearby room. Still stunned, the staff person did not know what was going on. She thought they might be other staff persons unknown to her, and for some reason in costume. While she debated what to do, the two figures peeked around the doorway. When they saw her still standing there, they jumped in fright and pulled back into the room. Gathering her courage, the staff person walked down to the other room and looked inside. It was empty. There was no other way out. For a brief few minutes, two time periods may have come together, with the parties in both eras left with an eerie experience.

You will note in the various stories that certain phenomena accompany time slips: a sudden change of environment to one unfamiliar to the percipient; a pronounced feeling of unease or depression; a weird silence – no bird or animal sounds, no commonplace background noises; an atmosphere that is "still" or "dead," or occasionally "electrical"; sometimes sudden changes in weather, including storms, fog and mist; and missing time.

Time Travel Mechanics provides discussion of the physics of time travel and how it might be undertaken. Can we overcome paradoxes such as "the grandfather paradox"? According to that scenario, what would happen if a person went back in time to kill his grandfather before his own father was born? Would he cease to exist? Perhaps he could return to a present but not the one he left; rather, it would have to be an alternate, parallel world. Among the articles is an exclusive interview with physicist Michio Kaku.

Lost in Time and Space is a fascinating collection of accounts of people who came from nowhere, people who mysteriously disappeared, places that no longer exist yet can be visited, and a defunct television station that continued to broadcast odd images and signals. It seems there are people and places wandering about time like the legendary Flying Dutchman.

Teleportation deals with individuals who experienced a sudden physical transport from one location to another – a slip in space that sometimes involved a slip in time as well.

The Bermuda Triangle and Devil's Sea features accounts of people who experienced strange anomalies and phenomena in highly charged areas of the Earth's oceans. Of particular interest is pilot Bruce Gernon's account of flying through a time warp while passing over the Bermuda Triangle.

The Philadelphia Experiment features one of the most controversial time travel episodes in history: the alleged disappearance and reappearance of a US Navy ship, the USS *Eldridge,* as part of a government experiment gone wrong. The case has been validated by some and debunked by others. Writer W. Ritchie Benedict weighs in with some interesting points to consider.

Included with some of the articles are photographs and drawings that were published in FATE. The originals no longer exist in the archives, and the quality of some of the images varies depending upon the paper quality of the magazine. FATE did not include author bios for all articles; where possible, they have been added at the end.

I know you'll be absorbed in this thought-provoking collection that may change your ideas about the nature of time.

– Rosemary Ellen Guiley,
Executive Editor, FATE

TIME SLIPS

A Night in Another Dimension

Jenny Randles

In October 1979, when Len and Cynthia Gisby and their friends, Geoff and Pauline Simpson, all of Dover, England, decided to take a trip, they certainly had no way of knowing precisely how far away they would be going. In fact, they were heading straight for one of the most baffling holidays of modern times.

Geoff Simpson, a railway worker, then 44, and his wife, then 45 and a cleaner at a social club, were quite excited when Len and Cynthia Gisby invited them to go along on their holiday trip. The plan was to take the ferry across the English Channel and drive through France to northern Spain for two weeks of late summer sunshine. Indeed, it all worked out perfectly. The weather was fine and the ride through the strange countryside was packed with interest.

On October 3, around 9:30 PM, they were on the autoroute (freeway) north of Montelimar, France, far to the south. It had been a pleasant day, but they were tired, and the encroaching darkness led them to look for a place to stay. Ahead loomed a plush motel and after a short discussion they decided to stop there for the night.

When Len went inside, he was confronted in the lobby by a man dressed in a rather strange plum-colored uniform. But he presumed this to be part of the local custom. The man informed Len that unfortunately there was no room at the motel. "However," Len was told, "if you take the road off the autoroute there" – and he pointed south – "then you will find a small hotel. They will have rooms."

Len thanked the man and his party drove away. The last faint traces of daylight still painted the sky when they found the road indicated. As they drove on, Cynthia and Pauline commented on the old buildings lining the roadside. The posters plastered on them were promoting a circus. "It was a very old-fashioned circus," Pauline remarked. "That's why we took so much interest."

The men were more interested in the road itself, cobbled and very narrow. When no other traffic passed by, they began to doubt the wisdom of this plan. But suddenly Cynthia spotted some lights and they pulled to a halt in front of a building by the roadside. It was long and low, with a row of brightly lit windows. There were some men standing in front of it. Cynthia got out but came back to the car saying, "It's not a hotel. It's an inn." So, they drove on, past a long border of trees which now lined the road.

Presently they reached two other buildings. One appeared to be a police station. The other had a sign saying "Hotel." Thankful that their journey was over, Len got out and went to ask for accommodations. He came back sighing with relief. "They have rooms." And so, the tired travelers unloaded their bags. It was about 10 PM; they estimated it had taken them about 10 minutes to reach the hotel from the autoroute motel. The hotel itself was a curious ranch-style building. It had just two stories and looked quaint and old-fashioned. As they entered, two boys were just leaving.

Because none of the four spoke French and the hotel manager apparently spoke no English, they made themselves known as best they could and were shown to their rooms. On the way they noticed that the building's interior was as strange as its exterior. Everything was old and made of heavy wood. There were no tablecloths on the tables in the dining room and some men in rough clothes sat drinking around one table near the bar. There seemed to be no telephones, elevators or other modern equipment anywhere.

Upstairs in their rooms even odder delights awaited them. The beds were large but had no pillows, only bolsters. The sheets were heavy. The mattresses seemed to sag in the middle but felt comfortable enough to lie on. Besides, it was too late to go anywhere else. The doors had no locks, just wooden catches. And the two couples had to share a bathroom with old-fashioned plumbing and soap attached to a metal bar stuck in the wall. "Look at this funny soap," Geoff said, chuckling.

After unpacking they went down to the dining room for a meal. Although unable to understand the menu, they did recognize the word œuf (egg) and ordered four of that dish. After they had drunk lager from tankards supplied to them, their dinners arrived on huge heavy plates. Included with the eggs were steak and french-fried potatoes. Their meal finished, they drank more lager. The girl who served them could not understand English either, so they did not speak.

Satisfied with their meal and facing another long journey the next day, they went straight to bed. It took no time at all for them to fall asleep.

Morning woke them early; sunlight filtered in through the windows which had no glass in them, just wooden shutters. Pauline removed the chair she had wedged against the door because she was afraid to sleep without some way of holding the door shut. They dressed and went back down to the dining room for breakfast. This simple meal consisted of bread, jam and coffee. "The coffee tasted black and horrible," Geoff recalls with disgust.

While they were eating a woman came into the room and sat down opposite them. She wore a silk evening gown and carried a dog under her arm. "It was strange," Pauline says. "It looked like she had just come in from a ball, but it was seven in the morning! I couldn't take my eyes off her." Then two gendarmes arrived, wearing deep blue uniforms and capes and large peaked hats. "They were nothing like the gendarmes we saw anywhere else in France," Geoff says. "Their uniforms seemed to be very old."

As they finished breakfast they all decided they wanted some souvenir of this unusual hotel. They did not think of it as anything other than a charming rural place which would be a delight to talk about when they got home. So, Geoff took his camera into the room and photographed Pauline standing by the shuttered windows. Len, while out packing his car, took a photograph of Cynthia inside the hotel silhouetted against the window. Then, to be certain of at least one good shot, he took another one. His camera was sophisticated and had an automatic wind-on.

Len and Geoff decided to ask the gendarmes, who were still there talking to the manager, the best way to take the autoroute to Avignon and the Spanish border. But the policemen shrugged at the word "autoroute" and plainly did not know the term. Geoff presumed that Len's attempts at French dialect were just not successful.

Eventually the gendarmes understood that the travelers wished to go to Spain and directed them to the old Avignon road. From what little knowledge of the local geography they had, this seemed a long way round to the two Englishmen and they resolved to go back to the Montelimar autoroute by the way they had come.

With the car packed and all three companions ready to leave, Len went across to the manager and asked for the bill. The man scribbled a sum on a piece of paper and showed it to the rather astonished tourist. It read 19 francs (about $3.00).

"No, no." Len motioned. "For all four of us."

The manager simply nodded. When Len indicated that they had eaten a meal, the manager continued to nod. Len showed the piece of paper to the gendarmes who smiled and indicated that it was quite correct. Without further ado Len paid up in cash and they left.

"Come on," Geoff remembers whispering. "Let's get out of here before he changes his mind."

The day was hot and sunny, and they traveled the tree-lined road back to the autoroute quite easily. Again, it was deserted of traffic until they joined the road toward Spain. Then, forgetting all about the hotel, they went on to pass a very happy two weeks in Spain.

On the drive back, naturally, the four decided to stop at the same hotel. Not many places offered such unique service at such phenomenal prices. The weather was miserable, with rain bucketing down, but they found the turnoff easily and drove down it.

"There are the circus signs," Pauline called out. "This is definitely the right road."

But there was no hotel. They were concerned enough to return to the motel on the autoroute and ask directions. Not only did the man there know of no such hotel, but he denied any knowledge of the man in the plum-colored uniform who had directed them to it previously.

Three times they drove up and down the road. But there was no hotel! It had vanished into thin air.

By this time Cynthia was upset and crying. "It has to be here! It can't just disappear like that," she said.

Somebody else suggested it had been knocked down. "At those prices they probably went broke," one person speculated.

"They couldn't do that in two weeks. Not without a trace," Geoff concluded.

They finally gave up the hunt. Shaking their heads, they drove on north to Lyon and a hotel there. Bed, breakfast and evening meal for four, with admittedly rather more modern facilities, cost them 247 francs (about $40).

The Gisbys and the Simpsons were mildly intrigued by their adventure, but it never crossed their minds to invest the story with a paranormal explanation until their holiday snapshots arrived back. Geoff had a 20-exposure Kodak film and had taken it to a local chain store. Len had a 36-exposure film which had been processed by the manufacturer. The three photographs of the hotel (one by Geoff, two by Len) had all been taken in the middle of the respective films. But none of the hotel shots were returned. What's more, there were no spoiled negatives. Each film had its full quota of photographs. It was as if the pictures that they all clearly remember taking did not exist; they had disappeared into limbo just like the hotel!

Utterly baffled and confused, the four resolved to tell only their families and friends. Geoff, raised in Rochdale, Lancashire, visited his home in January 1980 and told his family. When I talked with them in 1985, they smiled but said, "If anyone else had told us we would have laughed. We still chuckled but we knew it had to be true."

A fashion-conscious friend discussed the uniforms with Len and pointed out from a book that gendarmes did wear the kind he was describing – prior to 1905! One or two persons suggested that they had experienced a "time slip" and stayed at a hotel which existed around the tum of the century. Len and Cynthia thought this idea made sense. Geoff and Pauline preferred to forget the whole thing.

But unbeknown to them, one person they talked to actually worked for the local newspaper in Dover. Three years after the events she published their tale and the cat was finally out of the bag. From then on, the publicity bandwagon began to roll.

Looking back, in July 1985, Geoff was philosophical. "We never wanted the publicity," he said. "We just wanted to forget it. But once it happened then we all wanted to go back and try again to find that hotel. This trip is the only thing we ever got out of it. A local TV station made a drama about it, but we never got paid. They jazzed it up, using actors like Gordon Jackson from *Upstairs Downstairs*. For instance, when it came to the photographs, they had us taking one picture of the group of us standing in front of the hotel. That never happened. Then, in the film, when the picture came back, we were in it, but the hotel wasn't. That's just eyewash. Why do they do things like that?"

In 1984 Yorkshire Television, filming the series *Arthur C. Clarke's World of Strange Powers*, flew the four of them to Lyon and then filmed reconstructed attempts to find the hotel. "They set it all up by getting the police to pretend to call the tourist board. But we did go to the area and look. We even thought we had found the place. But it was not our hotel – just an old house – nothing like the hotel. At the place where we were all sure the hotel had been there was nothing at all."

The French tourist board in Lyon says there is no hotel like the one the Gisbys and Simpsons describe.

Geoff and Pauline were adamant that, apart from this trip, they had never made any money out of their story. "We don't want to," they say. "We just know it happened."

Yorkshire TV personnel say they examined Len Gisby's camera and film negatives. "There was evidence that the camera had tried to wind on in the middle of the film. Sprocket holes on the negatives showed damage." But of the mysterious photographs there was no trace.

In July 1985 I spent an evening with the Simpsons, in the company of fellow researchers Linda Taylor and Harry Harris. Harris had arranged for the couple to be interviewed and hypnotically regressed by psychiatrist Dr. Albert Keller at his Manchester surgery. Pauline could not be hypnotized but Geoff Simpson proved an excellent subject, reliving the events with emotion and awe. A detailed description of the adventure was offered but no new elements were uncovered (or fantasized).

What really happened to the four travelers in rural France? Was this a time slip? If so, one wonders why the hotel manager was apparently not surprised by their futuristic vehicle and clothing and why he accepted their 1979 currency (which certainly would have appeared odd to anybody living that far back in the past). The Simpsons consider these points and have no explanations.

"You tell us what the answer is. We only know what happened," Geoff concludes.

Jenny Randles: Author and former director of investigations with the British UFO Research Association; investigator of paranormal phenomena; author of Time Storms: The Amazing Evidence of Time Warps, Space Rifts and Time Travel *(2001).*

FATE January 1986

A Slip in Time and Place

Mary Rose Barrington

Personal experiences provide the case material that makes psychical research such a richly complex field of study. This report concerns a shared visual, auditory and tactile hallucination. The case was originally reported to the Society for Psychical Research in London in 1956. Because the SPR was involved in moving, no action was taken on the story. But in 1973 the couple who shared the adventure learned of my interest in psychical research and told me their story.

During the summer of 1954 Mr. and Mrs. George Benson (pseudonyms) were preoccupied with an exhibition which was taking up most of their time. They had been married for five years and were antique dealers. Being overworked and generally worn out, they decided to give themselves a day off and spend a whole Sunday walking in the Surrey hills.

But when they got up early on the scheduled morning, Mrs. Benson was afflicted by a feeling of black depression. Not wanting to spoil the day's outing, she said nothing to her husband about how she felt.

After the couple returned home to London later that day, her husband admitted that he too had awakened depressed.

The Bensons originally intended to get off their country bus at the Rookery, a few miles along the main road which runs between Dorking and Guildford. Although they knew the district intimately, they missed the stop and didn't get off until the next one at Wotton Hatch. Their first inclination was to make their way back to the Rookery on foot, but they decided instead to spend some time at the Evelyn family church at Wotton. The church lies at the end of a minor road on the north side of the main road from Dorking.

The couple ended up spending more time at the church and in the churchyard than they had originally intended, most of the time inspecting tombs and reading their inscriptions. They noted that this was the first time they had ever found the gates to the tomb inside the church open.

When they came out of the churchyard gate sometime later, they turned right and found themselves facing an overgrown path, bordered by high bushes on either side. Following the path, they climbed for a considerable time and finally came to a wide clearing where there was a wooden bench. To the left of the bench was an expanse of grass, with woodlands lying about 25 yards away behind it. To the right was a steep falling-away of the land. Mrs. Benson later said she felt sure about the height of the location because the view was consistent with a view from a hill and "down in the valley below" she could hear what sounded like wood being chopped as well as the monotonous barking of a dog. She felt uneasy, but she didn't know why.

As he sat on the bench, Mr. Benson glanced at his watch and observed with surprise that it was already noon. This prompted the couple to unpack the sandwiches they had brought along but Mrs. Benson felt too depressed to eat anything, so she started crumbling bread for the birds. Suddenly all became silent and the birds seemed to stop singing. Mrs. Benson started to feel cold and was overwhelmed with fear. Then she "saw" three figures standing in the clearing.

She was aware mostly of their faces and dimly perceived that they were wearing black clerical garb. The man in the middle had a roundish, friendly sort of face but the two on either side of him radiated hatred and hostility. She felt sure that these figures somehow belonged to the past. But what she found especially frightening was that the clearing in which

The church in Wotton, Surrey

they stood was behind her; in other words, she could "see" these figures without turning her head! When she did try to turn around, a sense of paralysis prevented her from doing so.

An icy coldness enveloped her. She was so uncomfortable that she asked her husband if everything had gone cold. He felt her arm and remarked that she felt like a corpse. Eventually Mrs. Benson "unfroze." As soon as she did, she told her husband that they had to get out of there. Mr. Benson, well aware that his wife had undergone some sort of unpleasant experience, was more than willing to move on. They walked a little farther and began to descend from the rise. Soon they were on one of the paths that crossed a local railway line and they walked over it.

They never did take their planned walk. At this point, in true fairy tale tradition, they lay down and went to sleep! To this day they do not remember leaving the area and cannot say whether they walked back to Dorking or returned to the road to take the bus. All they recall is that they arrived back at Dorking some hours later and took the train home to Battersea.

13

So far you might be thinking that this type of "haunting" experience is not unusual enough to warrant any special attention. It is odd, though, that Mr. Benson, although he never saw or even sensed the three figures, was overcome by the same subsequent fatigue and amnesia that afflicted his wife. But the truly bizarre features of this case were still to come to light.

Over the next two years Mrs. Benson never entirely recovered from the intense fear she had felt when she saw the three figures in the clearing. The experience practically obsessed her, and she came to believe there was something about the experience she had to face and overcome. So almost exactly two years later Mrs. Benson set out by herself for Wotton with the intention of revisiting the church, the churchyard, the entry to the shrub-surrounded path, the hillside and the bench at the top.

By the time she arrived at the churchyard she already sensed that things were strangely different. She headed for the church, looked around inside, wandered around the tombstones and returned to the gate. She turned right after coming out of the gate, naturally expecting to come to the path leading to the hillside. But there was no path! There was nothing even remotely resembling the hillside that she and her husband remembered climbing. Some woods lay half a mile to the west but like the rest of the land, these were low-lying. Flat field lands extended mostly around the area, while an open grass slope descended to the east.

She was so taken aback that she sought out a local resident who claimed that he knew the area well and that he couldn't think of *anywhere* that looked like the scene she described to him – with the overgrown ascending path and the woods-backed grass clearing at the top of the plateau. Nor did the man know of any wooden bench. He insisted that such a landscape was not to be found anywhere near the church.

Mrs. Benson returned home and told her husband about her remarkable visit. Unable to believe her, he vowed to investigate the situation himself. The next Sunday he visited the church, arriving at around noon as the congregation was beginning to leave. He approached someone who turned out to be a woodsman on the Wotton estate. Mr. Benson described the area (the vanished landscape) he had seen during his previous visit and asked the woodsman if he could think of any local site that filled the description. The woodsman said he couldn't and went on to state categorically that there were no wooden seats or benches on the Wotton estate – and that, so far as he knew, there never had been.

What are we to make of this extraordinary tale? It seems to be a unique case in which apparitional figures (seen by only one witness) were grafted onto a phantom landscape experienced by two persons. The expression "phantom landscape" is hardly appropriate, however, because the Bensons did not merely observe the scene. They climbed up on it, sat on a phantom bench within it and ate there too.

If the figures were contemporaneous with the landscape, we can only conclude that the Bensons spent their strange afternoon not only in the wrong place but in the wrong time as well. It is unfortunate that the figures were draped in black; if they had been clothed differently, we might be able to determine the historical context in which they may have existed. It seems clear enough, however, that they did not belong to July 1954.

Could the Bensons have been mistaken about their experience? Could a more diligent search locate the vanished landscape? To investigate these possibilities, I decided to look into the Bensons' case personally. In 1973, together with John Stiles, a fellow member of the Society for Psychical Research, I spent several hours in the Wotton area looking for Mrs. Benson's ascending path, tree-backed clearing and wooden bench.

Our on-the-spot investigation confirmed the story the Bensons had reported, for we were able to see soon enough that the land around Wotton church is definitely flat. (The only exception is the grass slope at the back.) It was difficult for us to imagine that the scene might ever have looked otherwise even in the past.

We also inspected the landscapes surrounding other churches in the vicinity but concluded that this was a useless endeavor. It seems unlikely that the Bensons were mistaken about which church they had visited, especially since they had examined the Evelyn family tombs which identified the church without question. It is possible that the Bensons' mysterious landscape exists somewhere in the Surrey hills, but it would take a gifted diviner or more than ordinary luck to find it.

We eventually made two further expeditions to the area without much luck. On the second visit we found an overgrown ascending path leading to a small clearing about a quarter of a mile east of the church. Later, when we took Mrs. Benson there, she declared this could not possibly be the location she had experienced in 1954. She seemed genuinely disappointed that we had not solved the mystery.

In short, there does seem good reason to assume that the Bensons experienced a psychic event. Their whole day's activities were infused with something mysterious: their early morning depression, the phantom landscape, the strange sleep into which they fell after visiting the church and the daze during which they managed to get back home.

But the most important element of the mystery may be the three figures Mrs. Benson sensed. If we can identify them, perhaps we can "solve" the enigma of the couple's apparent retrocognitive experience.

Through long experience investigating psychic phenomena, I have learned that coincidences, although not paranormal in themselves, often manifest around a paranormal event.

From talking with the Bensons, I learned that it was their strong literary interests that first led them to the Evelyn church. They were interested in the life of John Evelyn, a 17th-century diarist whom they found to be a sympathetic figure. Only a few weeks after their visit, the couple received a letter from a descendant of the diarist. He was writing because of an upcoming literary festival and of course Mrs. Benson wanted to meet him to tell him about her experience at the church.

When they met, the descendant was immediately able to identify the round-faced, friendly man in the clerical garb whom Mrs. Benson had seen. He was identified as a character called "Soapy Sam," more properly known as Bishop Wilberforce, who died under mysterious circumstances in Deerleap Woods. (This is roughly the location of the Bensons' experience.) This was the first Mrs. Benson had ever heard of the bishop.

We found further clues to the nature of the Bensons' experience when we examined other cases of shared visions. The only account I know of that is similar to the story the Bensons told me appears in C. G. Jung's autobiographical *Memories, Dreams, Reflections* (1963).

Jung's experience took place on his second visit to the tomb of the Empress Galla Placidia, for whom he felt a strong sympathy, in Ravenna, Italy. (The empress was a highly cultivated woman who was married off to a barbarian prince. Jung wondered how she could have endured her life with him.) His psychic encounter occurred in the baptistery, where he was surprised to find four mosaic frescoes of incredible beauty. These seemed to replace the windows he recalled from his first visit. The psychiatrist, who was accompanied on the trip by a friend, examined the frescoes for about 20 minutes and then the two visitors discussed them in some detail.

Only later, when the psychiatrist asked an acquaintance to photograph the frescoes for him, did Jung realize that he and his friend had shared a visionary experience. That realization came when he learned that the frescoes were not there, nor had they ever been there. His original memory of the four windows was the correct one after all and there was simply no trace of any mosaics at the tomb. Jung later discovered that Galla Placidia had once ordered the building of the basilica of San Giovanni (also in Ravenna) which had been adorned with mosaics. But fire had destroyed the basilica sometime in the Middle Ages.

It is remarkable that Jung's experience took place in a location unalterably fixed by a tomb and that the personality of the tomb's occupant was firmly on his mind just before the paranormal event took place. Notice that this setting is precisely the one that may have triggered the Bensons' shared visionary experience at the Evelyn family church. The Bensons had been particularly interested in finding the gates of the tomb open, which enabled them to study the inscriptions before setting out on their walk.

While discussing his experience in his autobiography, Jung writes that Galla Placidia's tomb "seemed to me the final legacy through which I might reach her personally. Her fate and her whole being were a vivid presence to me; with her intense nature, she was a suitable embodiment of my anima." [Anima: the feminine side of a masculine personality.] The idea is echoed by Jung's colleague and editor Aniela Jaffe, who writes that "Jung himself explained the vision as a momentary new creation by the unconscious, arising out of his thought about archetypal intuition. The immediate cause of the concretization lay, in his opinion, in a projection of his anima upon Galla Placidia."

This hardly ranks as an explanation but nonetheless let us pursue this line of reasoning. If this sort of imaginative sympathy led Jung and his companion to see some mosaics that were once part of Galla's earthly experience, might it be possible that the Bensons' sympathy for John Evelyn caused them to experience some glimpse of life as he once perceived it? Going through the six volumes of Evelyn's diaries, I read Evelyn's description of himself as "wood-born"; his earliest childhood memory was of being put out to nurse "in a sweet place towards the hills, flanked with wood." He tells us that Wotton, where he was born, was "situated… upon a very great rising," although the manor house itself was situated on low ground. Evelyn loved the woods but when one of his brothers got deeply into debt, he was forced to turn most of the trees into timber. His only stipulation was that some woods close to the family house be left standing.

Perhaps in these passages are hints that the Bensons were sharing a glimpse of Evelyn's earthly experiences, not on the exact site (any more than were Galla's mosaics) but in the general Wotton area. But Evelyn could not have had a vision of Bishop Wilberforce among his memories; the bishop was born some 100 years after the diarist's death. The most significant entry in Evelyn's diaries, however, is an entry dated March 15, 1696, in which he first notes with approval the sermon delivered that day at Wotton church by the curate. This entry is followed by another that records the execution of "three unhappy wretches, whereof one a priest," who were part of a Catholic plot to assassinate King William. Could these "unhappy wretches" have been the three Mrs. Benson saw?

I suggest that the Bensons' shared vision was of a deviant reality in which they momentarily sojourned. Such a deviant reality may differ from accepted reality by degree rather than in kind. I even suspect that such experiences take place more frequently than the occasional recorded accounts suggest.

In our usual way of looking at the world we assume that the sequence of events we experience in our day-to-day lives represents reality. If two or more persons experience events inconsistent with the mainstream, we say that they are hallucinating. But this interpretation may be simplistic. My speculation is that one day 30 years ago Mr. and Mrs. Benson deviated from their perception of "consensus" reality and were able to bend reality temporarily into a new shape. The causes for their psychic journey remain unknown but perhaps they were connected with the couple's depression, exhaustion and preoccupation with John Evelyn and his life.

But let's end this discussion with a question: If a third person had come out of the Evelyn church that afternoon, would he have walked into a flat field? Would he have been caught up in the special reality being created or experienced by the Bensons? Or would his more conventional perceptions of the vicinity have short-circuited the Bensons' experience? If such were the case, perhaps it is lucky that he wasn't around. His prosaic presence would have deprived us of some fascinating grist for parapsychology's ever-open mill.

Mary Rose Barrington: Parapsychologist, author, former barrister and former president of the Oxford University Society for Psychical Research. She joined the Society for Psychical Research, London, in 1957, serving as Council member and vice-president.

FATE October 1985

Bumps on the Time Track

Brad Steiger

Some years ago, a friend of mine from Aurora, Illinois, told me of the time that he had stayed overnight in a haunted house on a dare from his fraternity brothers.

"I was about to write the whole thing off as the dullest night in my life," Bill said, "when I heard noises in the front hallway. At first, I thought it was some of my frat brothers sneaking around to scare me. I stepped away from my sleeping bag in a front room to come face-to-face with a man in a belted smoking jacket about to start up the stairs."

The man seemed as startled as Bill. He blinked his eyes, shook his head as if to clear his senses, then continued on his way up the staircase.

"When he was almost at the top, the man slowly turned around and looked down at me. We had eye contact for several seconds before the man resumed his movement up the stairs and walked through a wall."

Bill was confident that he had seen a real ghost. Later he learned that there had once been a door to a bedroom at the very spot where the phantom had walked through the wall.

I agreed that he may have seen a ghost, but I suggested that Bill may also have briefly stepped into another dimension in time (possibly the early 1900s, judging by his description of the man's clothing) and encountered a former resident on his way to bed. Apparently, the startled gentleman in his era also saw a "ghost" and he may have talked for the rest of his life about the wraith of a tall, thin youth with shoulder-length hair and a beard that he encountered one night at the foot of the stairs.

In numerous cases that I have investigated, I have often wondered if the witnesses have truly encountered ghosts or if they suddenly stepped into a restored scene from the past – and for a time they, themselves, became "ghosts" out of time and space.

In other instances, witnesses may have met the spirit of someone who remains as attached to a place in death as he or she was in life, thus by will defying the mortal limitations of time and space.

Encounter in the mountains

Neville, one of my correspondents from Australia, told me of the time when he took his friend Angie to see Mushroom Rocks, a place situated halfway up Mt. Erica in the state of Victoria:

"One has firstly to drive up a winding road to a parking area, then hike up a narrow pathway for another hour to reach the huge boulders of Mushroom Rocks. When we reached the parking area on the climb up the mount, we were surprised to see an early model car sitting parked to the side. I was driving a four-by-four, and it was a difficult enough trip for me, yet this old model car managed to get up there apparently without a problem. I also noticed that the car was in pristine condition. It was raining that day and we had had several days of driving rain prior to that day – yet this car was totally clean."

Suddenly an elderly gentleman appeared just ahead of Neville and Angie on the walking path. He was dressed in a clean brown tweed suit and wore brown leather shoes. Neville remembered thinking how inappropriate his clothing seemed for a hike up to Mushroom Rocks.

"Angie and I were dressed for hiking in heavy boots, jackets, and hats, plus both of us were carrying backpacks and walking sticks. The hike ahead of us was treacherous, to say the least."

The elderly man in the brown tweed suit told the couple that he had just been to the dentist and had some teeth removed. He had decided to go on a hike in the mountains to help himself recover from the trauma.

"We were at least 40 miles from any dentist, way out in the forest, halfway up a mountain, yet here he was," Neville said. "Why would anyone who wanted to recover from a visit to the dentist travel so far in the bush and to such a strange place as this?"

The man then went on to advise Neville and Angie about the damage that the bad weather had done to the walking path, and he warned them about a tree that had fallen across the trail.

"I kept looking at his shoes and noted that they were perfectly clean, not a sign of mud on them at all. How could he have hiked up the path to the Rocks and returned without getting his shoes muddy?"

They said their goodbyes to the gentleman, then proceeded to head up the mountain trail. The whole way up, Angie and Neville discussed the strangeness of their encounter with the kindly old man in his tweed suit.

"I listened for the sound of his car leaving the parking lot, but I heard nothing, even though sound carried very well in that area. About halfway up the steep trail, we found the fallen tree across the path, and we wondered again how the old man could have walked up the rugged track in a suit without getting his shoes dirty."

When the couple returned to the parking area after their ascent and return from the Rocks, Neville examined the area where the old man had parked his car to see if he had left any sign. Although the ground was wet and muddy, he found no trace of the man's car tires.

"There were also no footprints from him at all. Yet our footprints were all over the place."

Neville offers the following as a final twist to his story and as a possible explanation of the mysterious appearance of the man in the brown tweed suit: "When Angie and I reached the Mushroom Rocks, we walked straight up to a specific outcrop of huge rocks, and I noticed a brass plaque that commemorated a man who was instrumental in making the area open to tourists. Although the gentleman had died many years previously, Angie and I wondered if our encounter with the man in the tweed suit was actually the person named on the plaque, welcoming us to his pet project."

Welcome to Amarillo

When we are dealing with the mysteries of time and space and the unseen world beyond death, we may also encounter friendly spirits who maintain a passion for helping and advising people.

In October 1974, Rick decided to leave the cold weather of New York, pack all his belongings in a U-Haul, and head for the Southwest.

Driving down I-40, Rick entered Texas and decided to take a break just east of Amarillo:

"I found a quaint looking diner on a spur of the old Route 66 just off I-40. When I pulled in, a plump older woman came out of the diner and asked if I needed gas. I had to chuckle at the set of old pumps and the image of the elderly woman pumping gas. I told her I didn't need any gas, but I sure could use something to eat."

As Rick ate a delicious home-style meal of Texas cooking, the woman asked him where he was going. He told her that he was looking for a place to relocate, possibly in Texas, but he had no definite plans. "The elderly woman, looking for all the world like a chubby cherub, started to speak to me in a kind, motherly way. She was very encouraging and really helped build up my confidence. She told me that I would do just fine in Amarillo and that I should drive into town and take some time to look around."

Rick thanked her for the advice, and as he got up to leave, she followed him out to his car. "You'll do just fine in Amarillo," she said again. "You'll settle here for a good long while and you'll start a new life."

Touched by her motherly concern and inspired by her confidence, Rick drove into Amarillo. On his second day in the city, he got a great job with Bell Helicopter Company and he rented a house. The company was located at the Amarillo Airport off I- 40 on the city's east side.

"After several weeks on the job, I decided one day that I would drive out to the diner and see the nice old woman who had been so kind and who had offered me so much encouragement when I needed it most. I wanted to thank her for her inspiration and tell her how things had worked out so great, just as she had predicted."

Since he had lived in Amarillo for quite some time at this point, Rick knew his way around the city. He drove east until he found the spur off old Route 66 where he knew the diner was located. At first, he thought he had somehow missed the quaint diner with its antiquated gas pumps, so he drove about 20 miles east, then drove back again, looking for the place.

"All that I could find was an old road that had once been part of Route 66, but there were no structures left on it," Rick said.

Discouraged, Rick drove home. The next day at work, he asked a couple of friends who had grown up in Amarillo about the old diner east of town. Both of his friends agreed that there hadn't been any businesses open east of town since the early 1960s.

"I looked again and again, but I never found that diner and I never got to thank that sweet, cherubic old woman. I think, though, in some way, she knows how things turned out. I stayed in Amarillo for seven years, and 1 did start a new life."

Lost in the museum

Dogma has no place in our investigations into the paranormal. Sometimes we encounter cases in which the witnesses themselves disappeared, reappeared, and may have encountered entities from another dimension in their sudden and unexpected journey. At this moment in time and space, no one can fully explain such experiences as the following:

In February 2004, Jean and her husband Bob stopped to visit a tourist attraction in a Midwestern city. They arrived at the small museum at 3 PM, and they each went off in a different direction so that they might enjoy the displays at their own individual pace. Jean said that she had it timed mentally so she would be finished reading the placards and examining the exhibits by 5 PM, just as the museum was closing.

As she neared the last of the exhibits, she was approached by a man dressed in a trench coat and pulling a silver briefcase on a luggage cart. Jean wondered briefly why he would be toting a briefcase through a museum, but she directed her attention toward the display in front of her, which contained a video playing scenes from the 1960s.

The man in the trench coat watched the video in silence for a few moments, then said, "Hmmm. Sounds a lot like today, doesn't it?"

Without indicating whether or not he hoped to elicit a response from Jean, the man walked away, pulling the silver briefcase behind him.

A few minutes later, Jean walked out of the display area, almost exactly two hours after she had entered it.

Bob came running up to her, obviously quite upset. "Where have you been?" he demanded. "I was just about to call the sheriff and report you missing!"

Jean was shocked by her husband's anger. She told him that she had been in the museum the whole time.

Bob shook his head in firm contradiction. He said that he had been through the entire museum several times looking for her and had not even caught a glimpse of her. Puzzled, Bob had enlisted the help of staff members of the museum to search for her. No one had seen her.

Jean protested that she had seen Bob rushing through the displays on one occasion, but he appeared not to see her. She said that she had also noticed several staff members walking around the exhibits, but they had not paid any attention to her. How could Bob and the museum staff claim that they had not seen her when she had so clearly seen them? And how could they think that she could disappear in such a small building?

Jean asked about the man in the trench coat pulling the briefcase who had exited from the exhibits shortly before she had, but neither Bob nor any member of the staff saw such a person enter or leave the museum.

Earlier, several members of the staff had walked through the museum one final time and declared absolutely that there was no sign of anyone in the exhibit areas. Just as Bob was about to notify the authorities that his wife had disappeared, Jean emerged from the museum.

Where had she been for two hours? Why was she invisible to others? She could see her husband and members of the museum staff. Why couldn't they see her? And who was the strange man in the trench coat, who apparently did see her and even spoke to her?

Jean is a well-educated woman, a staff member of a major university. She also has an interest in the paranormal, and she theorizes that "when objects from a different era are displayed in a concentrated area, perhaps the energy begins to shift." Could she, Jean wonders, somehow have been caught in that energy? She could see people; they evidently could not see her.

So many questions to answer. As Jean walked about the museum, engrossed by the exhibits, could she have entered a lightly altered state of consciousness, a kind of trance, which facilitated her entering another point in the Eternal Now of time? Or was the whole event a kind of psychic mechanism that allowed her to encounter her guide, who appeared as the man in the trench coat pulling the briefcase, and was really designed to open herself to more profound visionary experiences? Whoever he was, man or messenger, he apparently occupied the same dimension that Jean was visiting for those mysterious lost hours in a tourist museum.

Of one thing we may be certain; we are all potential mystics and shamans, and we may all one day expect our own encounter with the Great Mystery.

Brad Steiger (1936-2018): Author of more than 100 books on the strange and unknown; frequent contributor to FATE.

FATE December 2004

Breaking the Time Barrier

Hans Holzer

What this article is not

What I am about to share has nothing to do with out of the body experiences – astral projection – where a person seemingly journeys from out of the body to other, actual places, observes people and things at that distant location, and then returns to the body. OBEs are not hearsay or fiction, they are a common psychic experience that people have reported in large numbers.

This is not "distant viewing" or, as Eileen Garrett called it, "traveling clairvoyance" where the mind reaches out like a kind of radar to gather information. This is plain, simple astral projection of the inner body out of the physical body and then returning to it again.

Nor does what I am about to report have anything to do with psychometry, the ability by many to relive the past through extrasensory perception. Psychometry is essentially a mental experience confined to the thought perception processes within the mind of the perceiver. It is a little like watching a movie inside your head. Perhaps more dramatic but basically also two-dimensional is the ability of deep trance mediums to relive past events first person rather than by describing them.

Only when a deep trance medium is able to let an earthbound person – a ghost, if you will – speak through the medium's vocal apparatus, do we partake of a kind of living experience rather than a description of events past. Again, I am not about to report another ghost story of any kind.

What I am reporting here, as the personal investigator of these amazing cases, is a rare and very puzzling phenomenon that does not fit into any of the aforementioned categories of psychic phenomena.

Recently, a FATE article called my attention to this story of a man and the town he visited which does not seem to exist on the objective plane (*National, Indiana*, FATE, February 1991—see elsewhere in this volume). This made me remember how on May 11, 1967, I was contacted by a reader of my books, Susan Hardwick of Philadelphia, Pennsylvania, who wanted to share an amazing experience with me in the hope of getting some explanations.

Susan's strange story

"In the summer of 1960 I took a ride with a friend, Sal Sassani, along my favorite route. This was Route 152, starting in Philadelphia as Limekiln Pike, a beautiful, winding, country road which goes way up into the mountains. I have traveled it for years and know every curve with eyes closed! About an hour after darkness fell, I sat stiff with a start: I knew we had not made an improper turn, yet the road was unfamiliar to me all of a sudden. The trees were not the same. I became frightened and asked Sal to make a U-turn. As we did so, we both smelled what to us felt like a combination of ether and alcohol. At the same time, the car radio fell silent! Suddenly we saw a shepherd puppy running alongside the car; his mouth was moving but no sound was heard. Then, from our right, where there was no real road, came a ghostly shadow of a long, hearse-like car. It crossed directly in front of us and disappeared. The odor vanished, and the radio came back on at the same time."

I responded with questions, and on May 23, 1967, she contacted me again. To my question as to whether she had ever had any other strange experience at that location, Susan Hardwick went on to report an earlier incident, which had apparently not been as frightening to her as the one later on.

Her second story

"In the summer of 1958 I was driving with a friend, Jerry, on this same road, Route 152, and we turned off it onto New Galena Road. Halfway toward 611, which is parallel to 152, we came upon a wooden building I had never seen there before. We stopped and entered and sat at a table, and my friend Jerry noticed a man who resembled his late father. We each had a Coke. This man addressed us both by our names, calling Jerry 'son,' and told him things only Jerry's father would have known. Jerry became convinced it was his father. We left and drove on a road I had never seen before, yet I knew exactly what lay around every bend and curve! The incident took place about an hour from the city. I know exactly where this spot is, but I have yet to see this structure or these roads again."

I go to investigate

I decided to go to Philadelphia with famed medium Sybil Leek and investigate the case. On July 24, 1967, Sybil and I met up with Susan Hardwick and a friend of hers, Barbara Heckner. I had told Sybil Leek nothing about the case, but as we were driving toward the area I asked her if she received any kind of psychic impressions regarding it.

"This is not a ghostly phenomenon," she began, "this is a space phenomenon…we're going to cross a river." We were approaching Lancaster, Pennsylvania, and no river was in sight, but five minutes later we came to the river.

Sybil conveyed the feeling of masses of people in an open place, gathered for some reason, and she compared her feelings to an earlier visit to Runnymede, England, where people had once gathered to sign the Magna Carta.

We had reached the point 40 miles from Philadelphia where Susan had been twice before and experienced the inexplicable. What did Sybil feel about the location?

"It's a happening…not a ghost…in the past…two hundred years ago…*out of context with time*…I feel detached…like no man's land… we shouldn't be here…as if we were aliens in this country. I have to think what day it is, why we are here…it feels like falling off a cliff…I feel a large number of people in a large open space."

We began walking up an incline and Sybil indicated the vibrations from the past were stronger here. "We are in their midst now, but these people are confused, too."

31

"Why are they here?" I asked.

"Unity…that is the word I get, Unity."

I then turned to Susan Hardwick and asked her to point out exactly where her two experiences had taken place. This was the first time Sybil Leek heard about them in detail.

''When I drove up here in 1958 with my friend, this road we're on was not there. The road across from us was, and there was a building here, a wooden frame building that had never been there before. We felt compelled to enter somehow, and it seemed like a bar. We sat down and ordered Cokes. There were several men in the place and my friend looked up and said, 'That man over there looks like my father.' The man then spoke to us and called us by our first names as if he knew them. He began predicting things about my friend's future and called him 'son.''

"But didn't you think there was something peculiar about all this?"

"Yes, of course we did, because Jerry's father had died when he was a baby."

"Did everything look solid to you?"

"Yes, very much so."

"How were the people dressed?"

"Country people…work shirts and pants."

"Were the Cokes you ordered…real?"

"Yes. Real, modern Cokes!"

I looked around. There was nothing whatever in the area remotely looking like a wooden building. "You're sure this is the spot, Susan?"

"Definitely, we used to picnic across the road…that little bridge over there is a good landmark."

"What happened then?"

"We finished our Cokes, walked out of the place, got into the car and Jerry turned to me and said, 'That was my father.' He accepted this without any criticism. So, we drove off and came upon a road that I had never seen before and have yet to see again! I have tried, but never found that road again. Then I told Jerry to stop the car and told him there would be a dilapidated farm building on the left, around the bend in the road. We proceeded to drive around it and sure enough, there it was. Then I stated there would be a lake on the right-hand side…and there was, too."

"Did you ever find these places again?"

"Never. I am very familiar with the area…throughout my childhood I used to come here with friends many times."

"When you left the area, was there anything unusual in the atmosphere?"

"It felt rather humid...but it was an August afternoon."

"Did you go back later to try and find the place again?"

"Yes...we retraced our steps, but the building was gone. The road was still there, but no building."

'Was there anything in the atmosphere that was unusual when you wandered into that wooden bar?"

"Humidity...an electrifying feeling. Very cool inside."

"The people?"

"The man who seemed to be Jerry's father, the bartender and several other men sitting at the bar."

"Any writing?"

"Just signs like 'sandwiches' and different beer signs."

I thought about this for a while. Was it all a hallucination? A dream? A psychic impression? Susan assured me it was not. Both she and Jerry had experienced the same things. Neither had been asleep. "What about the people you met inside this place? How did they look to you?"

"Solid...they walked...and...that was the funny thing...they all stared at us as if to say, 'who are you, and what are you doing here?'"

"When you first drove up here and noticed that the area was unusual, did you notice any change from the normal road to this spot?"

"Only where the stop sign is now. That did not exist; instead there was gravel and that wooden building. It started right in from the road, maybe 50 feet from the road. Further back it was as normal as it is today. Suddenly it was there and the next moment we were in it."

I decided to go on to the second location, not far away, where Susan's other experience had taken place in the summer of 1960. Again, as we approached it, I asked Sybil for any impressions she might have about the area and incident. Even though this was a different location, though not too far from the other place, Sybil felt that "the strength of the force is constant" between the two places. But she did not feel any of the odd excitement she had earlier picked up en route to, and at, the first location.

Once again, Susan pointed out the clump of trees she remembered from the incident. "We were riding on this road," Susan explained, "a road, by the way, I have known for many years firsthand. It must have been around midnight, in the middle of July in 1960. All of a sudden, this stretch of the road *became extremely unfamiliar.* The trees were not the same anymore. They looked different, much older than they are now. There were no houses here, just completely open on the right side of the road."

There are small houses in the area she points to. "This clump of trees was very thick, and out of there where today there is no road, there was then a road. All of a sudden, on this road came a ghost car, like a black limousine, *except that you could see through it.*"

In her earlier letter to me she had mentioned the peculiar smell of what seemed to be ether and alcohol mixed, and the car radio had stopped abruptly. At the same instant, she and her friend Sal saw a German Shepherd puppy run alongside their car, with his mouth moving but without any sound, no barking being heard! "How did the dog disappear?" I asked.

"He just ran off the road when the black limousine pulled out in front of us – a hearse I'd say. There is a cemetery right in back of us, you know."

There still is.

But as Susan and Sal were driving in the opposite direction from the one they had come from, the hearse was going away from the cemetery, not toward it. "What about the driver of the hearse?" I queried.

"Just a shadow. The hearse went alongside our car and then suddenly vanished. The whole episode took maybe seven or eight minutes. We drove back toward Philadelphia, very shook up."

Rather than drive on through the strange area of the road, they had decided to turn around and go back the other way. Now it was our turn to turn around and head back to the city. For a while we sat silent, then I asked Sybil Leek to speak up if and when she felt she had something to contribute to the investigation.

"I think if you stayed in this area for a week you wouldn't know what century you're in." Then she suddenly said, "I feel very confused… almost as if we had entered into another time, and then somebody pushes you back…as if they did not want you. This is a very rare situation… probably higher intensity of spiritual feeling…"

I turned to Susan's companion, Barbara, and asked her about her impressions, both now and before. "An apprehensive kind of feeling came over me," she replied. "We were here just a week and a half ago again, when we came upon this side of the road, and it was…different…

it felt as if it was not normal. All along this run, as soon as we hit 152, through New Galena, I feel as if *I'm intruding*...as if I don't belong, as though this whole stretch of country were not in existence in my time. I've been out here hundreds of times and always had this odd sensation."

I investigate further

While neither Susan Hardwick nor her friends had ever attempted to research the history of the peculiar area of their incidents, I did.

First, I contacted the town clerk at Trumbauersville, Pennsylvania, because today that is the nearest town to the area. I wanted to know specifically if there ever was a village or a drugstore/bar/ restaurant of some sort at the junction of Highway 152 and New Galena Road, not far from the little bridge which is still there. Also, I wanted to know the history of the area.

The reply came on March 1, 1968, from the director of the Bucks County Historical-Tourist Commission in Fallsington, Pennsylvania. "It is rural farm area now and has been from the beginning. From what I know about this area, and from *Place Names in Bucks County* by George MacReynolds and Davis' *History of Bucks County*, I know nothing of a drugstore in the area."

There was something else: Susan Hardwick reported finding some strange holes in the road in the area. "They seemed like [they were] left from the snow...filled with water...like a whirlpool. Many times, we stopped the car and put our hands into those potholes and we could not feel the road underneath them. We – my friends and I – stuck our arms into the holes and got wet. There was water in them. But when we came back another time, there were no holes. No water. Nothing."

I find some possible solutions

This inspired me to search further in MacReynolds' *Place Names in Bucks County*, which also contains the detailed history of the area. Here is where I found at least a partial explanation for what these people had experienced along New Galena Road.

It appears that back in the 1860s, galena (lead sulfide) was discovered in this area and mines were started. Soon there was a veritable mini-gold rush for lead and some silver also, and people in the farm area began driving shafts into the earth to see if there was valuable ore underneath. Those must have been the "potholes" with water in them, but deep and "bottomless," which Susan and friends rediscovered – or at least their imprints from the past.

The town of New Galena became a mining center with all that this implied. Mining fever hit the rural population and turned farmers into speculators. By 1874 it was all over. Another attempt at exploiting the mines in the area was made in 1891 and as late as 1932 some work to restore railroad tracks to the mines was done, but it all came to naught. "Today the place is deserted," writes MacReynolds, "a ghost of itself in the boom days of the 1960s and 1970s."

This explains the strange feeling of not wanting "outsiders" intruding into their own mining bonanza, and it explains the water-filled shafts in the road. What it fails to explain is Jerry's father and the Coke bottles Susan Hardwick and Jerry drank from. I can only suggest that so intense an emotional fervor as that of a small, backward, rural community, suddenly caught up in a mining fever and dreams of great riches, might create a kind of psychic bubble in which it continues to exist in a time-space continuum of its own, separate from the outside world – except for an occasional, accidental intruder, like Susan and her friends.

The strange case of Robert Cory

At about the same time, I heard of a parallel case through the late Ethel Johnson Meyers, trance medium and psychic reader. A friend of hers in California had communicated to her an extraordinary experience which she felt was so unusual I had better investigate it. On June 1, 1967, I sat opposite Robert Cory, designer and actor, living then on Elmwood Street in Burbank. At the time, Mr. Cory was 30 years old, and premonitions and dreams were accepted phenomena in his family, which was of Near Eastern extraction.

In 1964, Cory took a vacation trip by car to visit his future in-laws in Kennewick, Washington. His fiancée was with him, but he left her with her parents after a few days to drive back to Burbank by himself. His car was a 1957 Corvette in excellent condition, and Mr. Cory was an experienced driver. The fall weather was dry and pleasant when he left the state of Washington. It would be a 12-hour trip down to the Los Angeles area. Cory left Washington around 11:30 PM, and when he crossed the Oregon state line it was already dark. The weather had not changed, however. He started to climb up into the mountains on a long, winding road going south. About four hours after he had left Washington, around 3:30 AM, he was rounding a bend and with one fell swoop he found himself in a snowstorm! One moment it was a clear, dry, autumn night – the next, a raging snowstorm. It was unbelievable.

"I slowed down. I was frightened," he explained, still shuddering at the experience now. "The road was narrow, mountain on one side, a drop on the other." Cory got out of the car. He could drive no farther. It was ice cold and snowing. Then he saw in the distance what appeared to be a bright light, so he got back into the car and drove on.

When he got to the "light" it turned out to be a road sign, reflecting light "from somewhere." He was now on top of a hill, so he coasted downhill until the car came to a full stop. Cory looked out and discovered that he had rolled into some sort of village, for he saw houses. When he got out of the car he found himself on a bumpy street.

"What did this town look like?" I asked.

"It looked like a Western town. The road went through it, but the road now had bumps in it as if it were a road with much work done to it."

Cory discovered that the car would not go any farther, anyway, and he was glad to be in this strange place. One building had the word "hotel" on it, and he walked toward it on wooden sidewalks. He knocked at the door. Everything was dark, but the door was open, and he entered the lobby of the hotel.

He yelled for someone to come, but nobody did – yet there was a potbellied stove with a fire in it.

He moved near the stove to get warm. To one side he noticed a barbershop chair. In the back he saw a desk and a big clock. To his left he saw a phone booth. The phone was an antique – you had to crank to get action! He cranked it and cranked it. The noise he made worried him, so he took off his sweater and wrapped it around the box while cranking to keep the noise down. Nobody answered.

"So, what did you do next?"

"I went back to the stove, ready to go to sleep and maybe in the morning there would be somebody there to talk to. After all, they've got a fire going. There must be some life in the place. So, I lay down on a sofa, when I heard a rattling noise coming from what looked like a cardboard box in a corner. I figured it might be a snake and got real worried. The heat, however, was putting me to sleep. I was exhausted and so I just fell asleep. I woke up due to some sound upstairs, and I saw a man coming down the steps, an old man of maybe 75, wearing big boots, which made the noise."

"What did he look like?"

"He wore old coveralls, like a farmer. Slowly he came down and to where the stove was. He sat down in a rocking chair across from it, and then he went to the men's room, or something, and again sat down. He saw me, and we nodded to each other. Then he kept on rocking while I was trying to get up courage to ask him some questions. Finally, he said to me, "You couldn't fall asleep…why don't you fall asleep?' I said, 'Well, that's all right, I'm not really tired, you know.' But he replied, 'No, you couldn't fall asleep, it's okay, it's okay.'"

"How did his voice sound?"

"Like an old man's voice, and as he kept saying over and over again, 'It's okay,' I fell asleep again. Once or twice I opened my eyes and saw him still sitting there. I slept till daybreak and when I woke up and opened my eyes, I saw eight or 10 men walking around, talking, doing different things. I sat up, but no one paid attention to me, *as if I were not there*. But I got up and said hello to one of them, and he said hello back to me. There were a couple men around the stove with their backs to me, talking, and then there was a man standing behind the barber chair *shaving somebody who wasn't even there*."

"Exactly what did you see?"

"He was shaving somebody, talking to him, moving his razor – but there was no one in that chair. He held up the invisible chin and carefully wiped the razor into paper. It was frightening to watch this. The razor was real, all right."

"Was there anything unusual about these people?"

"They seemed like normal people except I had the feeling they were in some way smaller. They all looked very old like the first man I saw coming down the stairs."

"What happened next?"

"One of the men was walking back and forth in the hotel lobby, talking to nobody, arguing, carrying on a conversation all by himself. So, I got up finally and looked outside. My car was still there, and the snow had stopped. There was no sign of life outside. I turned to the three men around the stove and asked, 'Is there a gas station around?' Now I could understand they were speaking to me, but the words made no sense.

"One of the men grabbed my wrist as if to point out a direction. Then I heard someone yell out 'breakfast.' I looked and noticed in the back of the lobby where the desk was, two doors were open now, leading into a dining room. Again, the voice yelled, 'Breakfast. Come, breakfast,' and this time the old man, the one I had seen first coming down the stairs, came over and grabbed my arm, saying, 'Come have breakfast.' I became so frightened I backed off and for the first time raised my voice, saying, 'No, thank you.'

"Everybody turned around and then they started to walk toward me, slowly, normally, not rushing. I said, 'Where am I? Where am I?' and the old man, who still held my arm, said, 'Don't worry. Don't worry.' But I turned and walked out and got into my car. I had forgotten about running out of gas."

"Did it work?"

"Yes, it did. I drove down this bumpy road and I saw the faces of the men looking out of the windows of the hotel behind me."

"Did you get a good look at these people? What did they look like?"

"Normal."

"You say he actually touched you. Did you feel it?"

"Yes, I certainly did."

"The clothes these people wore...were they of our time?"

"No, no. When I drove off I saw some more people in the street. One of them a woman...she wore a long dress like the Salvation Army women do."

"Describe what happened then as you left the place."

"I drove past the people on the sidewalk, and then there was something like a cloud I went through...like a fog...for about 30 seconds. Next thing I knew, I came out into one of the brightest, shiniest days you could imagine. I drove another half a mile or so until I saw a gas station, just in time. I was back in today's life."

"Did you question him about the place you had just left?"

"Here I was with a sweater, all buttoned up, and the attendant in short sleeves, bare chest out, sweating, and he gave me a funny look. I just couldn't tell him."

"Was there anything different about the atmosphere in that place you left?"

"Yes. I was very tense and nervous. But I was not dreaming this – I touched the sofa, I was fully awake."

I go to investigate – new details come out

At that point, Cory contacted his old friend Ethel Meyers and wrote down his experience for her. She in turn called me. I then looked at the original report which he gave to Ethel Meyers and realized he had left out some details when we met for the interview, three years later. Important details. Here they are:

When Cory arrived at the "hotel," there were six to eight inches of snow outside. He noticed wagons parked outside the hotel, wagons that hitch onto horses! He found this peculiar in this age. When he entered the lobby and looked around for the first time, Cory noticed animal heads on the walls, old furniture of another era, and a calendar on the wall dating back to the early 1900s! Also, some notices on a board on the wall with dates in the late 1800s. The telephone had a sign reading "CRANK BOX FOR OPERATOR." There was a clock on the wall loudly ticking. There were cats in one of the chairs, kittens to be exact. Apparently, there was more conversation between Cory and the old man. "Nice day isn't it?" he said and put his hand on Cory's shoulder. He said it felt more like "a chicken's foot."

Finally, when Cory drove off and looked back at the faces of the men in the hotel which were pressed up against the windows, he clearly noticed tears rolling down the face of "his" old man when Cory left.

Clearly, this is neither an imprint from the past nor a hallucination or ghostly apparition as we know them. The fog Cory drove through on his way "out" reminds me of the fog sometimes reported by people abducted by UFOs, or in connection with their landings.

My explanation

What happened here? I can only guess that somehow the combined energies of the people Cory encountered were strong enough, and their fear of leaving their little world powerful enough, to create this enclave in our time stream, forever keeping them from going on.

Original editor's note: Dominic P. Sondy, whose article, "National, Indiana," reminded Mr. Holzer about the above two strange incidents which he had previously investigated, sent us a copy of a letter which he mailed to Mr. Holzer. The letter reads:

"This is in response to your request that I enquire to the Indiana main post office to get more information about National, Indiana. I sent a letter to which I got no response. I then called and talked to a lady who was in charge of records. She gave me the following: National, Indiana, had a U.S. Post Office in 1850. This was taken over by a Veterans' Administration Hospital in 1930."

[The National, Indiana story appears in the "Lost in Space and Time" section.]

Hans Holzer (1920-2009): Paranormal researcher and author of more than 120 books.

FATE May 1991

THE VERSaILLES TIME SLIPS

Rosemary Ellen Guiley

One of the most famous time slip cases of the 20th century involved apparitions of people and buildings in the Petit Trianon at Versailles dating to the 1770s prior to the French Revolution. Reports of strange apparitions in the Petit Trianon were recorded as early as 1870, and Versailles became an important and controversial case for psychical researchers beginning in the summer of 1901.

Background

The Petit Trianon was intended by Louis XV for his mistress, the Marquise de Pompadour. The house was designed by Gabriel, the Royal Architect, and work on it began in 1762. In 1764, the Marquise died, and was succeeded as royal mistress by Madame du Barry. The house was finished in 1770, and Madame du Barry lived in it occasionally. A carriageway led to the Allee de la Menagerie, the king's small farm on the grounds.

Almost immediately upon completion, changes and additions were made. In 1773 a chapel was added to the house and replaced part of the kitchen and service premises. Steps leading to the kitchen door were replaced with new steps that served both the chapel and service doors. The chapel necessitated the closing of the carriageway, the southern end of which was obliterated by 1771. Louis XV died in 1774, and his grandson, King Louis XVI, gave the Petit Trianon to Queen Marie Antoinette, who quickly made plans for changes in the garden.

The time slip

On August 10, 1901, two English academics, Eleanor Jourdain, the daughter of a Derbyshire vicar, and Annie Moberly, the daughter of a bishop of Salisbury, visited Versailles. Neither was familiar with the layout of the immense palace grounds. They left the Grand Trianon and walked a long route toward the Petit Trianon and lost their way for a while. Upon finding the garden and entering it, Moberly suddenly felt what she later described as "an extraordinary depression." Both felt as though they were walking in a dream. The atmosphere was still, eerie and oppressed. The surroundings looked unpleasant, unnatural and flat, almost two-dimensional.

Versailles Palace

They saw two men, whom they took for gardeners, dressed in period costumes of grey-green coats and small tri-cornered hats. They asked the men for directions and were told to continue straight ahead. They saw a bridge and a kiosk. Near the kiosk sat a man in a slouched hat and cloak; for some reason, they disliked his appearance. A man with a "curious smile" and an odd accent ran up behind them and gave them further directions to the house; they thought he was one of the gardeners they had encountered at the entrance. He disappeared abruptly. Near the house, in the English garden in front of the Petit Trianon, Moberly saw a woman wearing a pale green fichu, sitting on a seat in the grass. Jourdain did not notice her. The attention of both women was drawn by a young man who came out a door of the house, banging it behind him. He looked amused, like the running man. They saw the carriageway to the house.

Later, in discussing their experiences on that day, Moberly and Jourdain concluded the Petit Trianon was haunted. They recalled that though a breeze had been blowing as they had departed the grounds of the Grand Trianon, the air had been "intensely still" upon their arrival at the Petit Trianon, and there had been no effects of light or shade. After encountering the two men in green, Moberly said, "I began to feel as if I were walking in my sleep; the heavy dreaminess was oppressive." The strange experience lasted about half an hour.

Aftermath

During the next 10 years, Moberly and Jourdain revisited the Petit Trianon in an attempt to unravel the mystery. On her second visit, on January 2, 1902, Jourdain once again encountered the heavy, eerie feeling, this time after crossing a bridge to the Hameau de la Reine. She saw two laborers, dressed in tunics and capes with pointed hoods, loading sticks in a cart. She turned aside for a moment, and when she looked back, she saw the men and cart were a great distance away. She also heard faint band music playing.

Moberly did not return a second time until July 4, 1904, accompanied by Jourdain and a French woman. They could not find the paths they had taken on their roundabout route in 1901, nor did they see the kiosk or bridge. Where they had seen the lady on the grass, they found instead an enormous rhododendron bush many years in

Petit Trianon

age. People were everywhere, whereas in 1901, the grounds had been strangely empty, save for the few persons they had seen.

After conducting historical research, Moberly and Jourdain believed they had seen visions of the Petit Trianon during the days of Marie Antoinette in 1789, and that the lady on the grass was the Queen herself, who reputedly liked to sit at that spot. Moberly theorized they had somehow entered into the Queen's memory when she had been alive. The clothing they had seen was not worn by any of the grounds staff in 1901; the door of the house, which the young man had banged, was in fact in a ruined and disused part of the chapel. The kiosk and bridge they had seen no longer existed. They identified the two gardeners as the Bersey brothers, who were attendants to Marie Antoinette.

Going public

Moberly and Jourdain wrote their experiences in a book, *An Adventure,* published in 1911. It earned them a great deal of derision from skeptics

46

in the psychical research community who criticized their research as unreliable and amateurish. They had not written down any recollections until November 1901, far too long a passage of time for memory to be certain, critics argued. The music heard in 1902 could have been one of the many military units which practiced maneuvers in the nearby area. The banging door could have been a sound nearby which they mistook for a banging door.

In reviewing the book, Eleanor Sidgwick, secretary of the prestigious Society for Psychical Research (SPR), stated that there did not seem to be sufficient grounds to prove a supernormal experience. Sidgwick proposed that Moberly and Jourdain had seen real persons and real things, the details of which became altered by tricks of memory after they decided they had seen ghosts.

More reports

Despite such criticism, *An Adventure* received wide publicity. Other Britons began reporting similar experiences in the Trianons to the SPR. John Crooke, his wife and son, of England, reported that in July 1908, they had visited the Grand Trianon and had twice seen "the sketching lady." The fair-haired woman was dressed in clothing of another century, a cream-colored skirt, white fichu, and white, untrimmed, flapping hat. She sat on a low stool on the grass and appeared to be sketching on a piece of paper. She paid no attention to them until Crooke, who was an artist, tried to see what she was drawing, and then she turned her paper away with a quick flick of her wrist. She seemed to be annoyed. The Crookes said later that at the time they believed her to be a ghost because the lady seemed to grow out of, and vanish into, the scenery "with a slight quiver of adjustment." The Crookes also reported seeing a man and another woman in old-fashioned dress, and hearing faint band music. The visions seemed to be accompanied by a vibration in the air.

Although the Crookes' experiences took place three years before *An Adventure* was published, critics were quick to point out that the family had said nothing until reading the book, and that therefore, their accounts were likely to have been influenced by what they had read.

Still other ghostly reports surfaced. In October 1928, two Englishwomen, Clare M. Burrow and Ann Lambert (later Lady Hay) visited Versailles. Neither had read *An Adventure*. They left the Grand Trianon and walked toward the Petit Trianon. Burrow felt a strange depression.

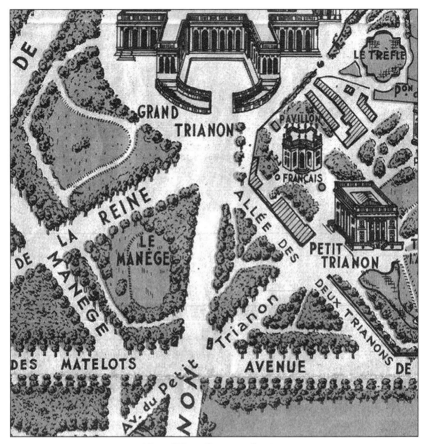

Map of Versailles grounds, 1920

They saw an old man dressed in a green and silver uniform and asked him for directions. He shouted at them in hurried, hoarse and unintelligible French. He suddenly seemed sinister, and the women hurried on. Looking back, they were astonished to see that he had vanished. They also saw men and women dressed in period clothing. When they spied the Petit Trianon through the trees, they were relieved. Later, Burrow read *An Adventure*, and felt she had also experienced a haunting.

In September 1938, Elizabeth Hatton walked alone through the grounds of the Petit Trianon, heading toward Marie Antoinette's village. Suddenly, a man and a woman in period peasant dress appeared about six feet in front of her, drawing a wooden trundle cart bearing logs. They passed by silently. Hatton turned to watch them, and they gradually vanished. Hatton had not read *An Adventure* before her visit.

On October 10, 1949, Jack and Clara Wilkinson took their four-year-old son to Versailles. All three saw a woman in period dress, with a parasol, standing on the steps of the Grand Trianon. She did not seem ghostly, but when they looked away and then looked back moments later, she had vanished.

On May 21, 1955, a London solicitor and his wife walked through the Trianons. As they left the Grand Trianon and headed toward the Petit Trianon, the grounds seemed strangely deserted. There had been a thunderstorm, and the air was heavy and oppressive. The wife felt depressed. Then the sun came out, and the couple saw coming toward them two men and a woman, who were about 100 yards off. They were dressed in period costumes. The woman wore a long, full dress of brilliant yellow, while the men wore black breeches, black shoes with silver buckles, black hats and knee-length open coats. The husband and wife conversed as they walked. Suddenly, they noticed the three persons had vanished – and there was nowhere for them to go that was out of sight.

Investigations

These and other reports were investigated by members of the SPR. Opinions as to the validity of the Versailles "ghosts" remained divided. Among the skeptics was W.H. Salter, who wrote in 1950 that faults of memory could not be excluded from the accounts. Salter observed that a public park is "about the worst setting for a ghost story" from the standpoint of evidence, for it is impossible to ascertain later exactly who was in a park, and where, at any given moment. He suggested that the period costumes seen were the dress of living persons, for Versailles attracted a colorful range of persons from various occupations and countries.

G.W. Lambert was more inclined to believe that paranormal events had taken place. He discovered that in 1775, the royal gardeners, Claude Richard, 65, and his son, Antoine, 35, wore green livery. Lambert proposed that the two men in grey-green seen by Moberly and Jourdain were apparitions of the Richards. Burrow, who had also seen a man in green, told Lambert that she estimated the man's age at around 60. Lambert found eight significant consistencies with what Moberly and Jourdain had seen. However, the conditions they described had existed at Versailles in the summer of 1770 during the reign of Louis XV – not during the days of Marie Antoinette, as the women had believed. Lambert's findings were published in a series of articles between 1953-62.

In 1965, the "Versailles Adventure," as it was called in the media, was given a natural explanation by Philippe Jullian in his book, *Un Prince 1900 -- Robert de Montesquiou.* Jullian said that Montesquiou, a poet, and his admirers were in the habit of spending days in the Trianon park at the turn of the century. Some apparently came in period costume, judging from existing photographs. Therefore, Moberly and Jourdain simply had witnessed Montesquiou and his friends rehearsing a *tableau-vivant* for an outdoor party.

Jullian's book had a great impact upon Dr. Joan Evans, who had inherited the copyright to *An Adventure,* in its fifth printing by 1955. Evans decided to put the matter to rest by prohibiting more English editions of the book.

The mystery continues

The matter, however, did not end. In subsequent years, more hauntings have been reported and examined by both English and French investigators. In 1982, Andrew MacKenzie, a member of the SPR, theorized that all the experiences fit a pattern of an "aimless haunting," which does not seem to be linked to traumatic or violent events. Life at Versailles was tranquil during 1770-71. MacKenzie suggested that the area acquired emotional power because its inhabitants of the time somehow sensed that their era was nearing an end.

The controversy over the validity of the Versailles experiences remains unresolved.

Ghosts or time slip?

Assuming that the eyewitnesses did indeed see people and scenes from the past, did they experience ghosts or time slips? Many places, especially of historical importance, are haunted by "residual ghosts," remnants of the past that exist like psychic photographs or videos. Residual ghosts usually do not interact with the living, or even seem aware of the living. Individuals who are in the right state of consciousness at the right time might perceive such ghosts. The Versailles palace and grounds are reportedly haunted by such residues.

However, the evidence points more to time slips. The apparitions were not superimposed on the present world; rather, the witnesses seemed transported back in time. What they saw appeared "real," not ghostly, and they had interactions with some of the strangers they encountered.

Various witnesses reported the eerie, still and unusual atmosphere – a characteristic of other apparent time slip episodes. Some of the witnesses had a sense of foreboding, also a time slip characteristic. Perhaps the area around the Petit Trianon exists in a "time vortex" that catches people under certain circumstances when personal and environmental conditions are ideal, and they are temporarily transported to another period in history.

Rosemary Ellen Guiley: Researcher and investigator in the paranormal and related fields; author of more than 65 books; executive editor of FATE.

2018

Time Distortions and the UFO Experience

Tim R. Swartz

For most people, spotting a UFO would be considered extremely unusual, but for two Ohio women, seeing a UFO was the least surprising part of their experience.

In June 2001, two sisters, Angie Whitmeyer and Deborah Simmons, were returning from a day of shopping in Dayton, Ohio, when a strange light in the sky caught their attention.

"We were heading home to Kingman, Ohio, on State Road 73," Deborah recalled. "It was a beautiful evening around 8:30 PM, the air was warm and the sky crystal clear. Angie was driving, and I was watching the scenery go by when I noticed a bright light in the western sky."

Deborah watched in amazement as the light grew in intensity and flew toward the car at an incredible speed.

"Deborah asked me what that weird light was," said Angie. "But we were close to Caesar Creek Lake and the road was pretty dark, so I wasn't paying a lot of attention to it. But then it flew right in front of us, so I couldn't miss it."

The bright light soared past the car and hovered over the nearby treetops, casting an eerie glow over the entire area. Angie pulled the car over onto the side of the road so they could get a better look at the unusual object.

Deborah was shocked by how large and close the UFO was to them: "The light was so bright and white that you couldn't see any shape behind it. But we could tell it was pretty big, at least as big as a house. The funny thing was that I couldn't hear any sort of engine like you would normally hear with an airplane or helicopter. It was completely silent."

Suddenly, another, identical bright light swooped down from the sky and hovered a short distance away. The two sisters decided the situation was becoming too strange and tried to drive away.

"That's when I discovered that the car had stopped, and I couldn't restart it," Angie said. "Nothing worked, the lights, the radio, it was completely dead."

The two women also noticed an odd silence had descended over the area, accompanied by a strange feeling of isolation. Angie remembered that it seemed as if they were the only people in the world.

"I don't remember seeing another car come by during the entire time we were there, which is really weird because at that time of an evening there's always traffic on that road. And it was just dead silent outside, no birds, nothing. It was as if we were in another world."

Uncertain what to do next, Angie and her sister continued to watch the strange pair of lights, when, unexpectedly, both objects shot straight up and disappeared into the night sky. The area was plunged into darkness, and oddly enough, the normal sounds of the night came back almost as if switched on.

"As soon as the lights flew away," Deborah said, "the car started running again all by itself. The lights and radio were on just as they were before everything happened."

According to their watches, the strange encounter had lasted more than 20 minutes. However, when they arrived home, Deborah's husband seemed unconcerned about what they thought was a late arrival. That's when they discovered that instead of being after 9 PM, as their wristwatches indicated, it was only 8:35 PM.

"It was as if the entire time we spent looking at those lights had never happened," Angie said. "But it did happen. Both our watches showed we had been stuck out there for over 20 minutes, but somehow we gained that time back with a few minutes to spare. Normally we should have been home at around ten to nine, but somehow, despite what had happened, we got there early."

Distortions in time and space

One of the strangest aspects of some UFO encounters is the apparent distortion of time when a UFO is nearby. Researchers and writers have tried for years to understand and to interpret what happens before, during, and after a close contact with a UFO. But, many reports of time anomalies have been kept off some UFO databases because such events fall outside of the preconceived notions of what a UFO sighting should entail.

Like the two Ohio sisters, others who have experienced a close contact with a UFO have reported apparent time distortions like the failure of car engines, a strange feeling of isolation (to the point where it is observed that no other vehicles or people are seen during the sighting), unusual silence, spatial changes, altered states of consciousness, and distortions in the flow of time.

Generally, these anomalies disappear along with the UFO. Occasionally, however, the witnesses will suffer from unexpected relapses weeks, even years, after the initial experience.

These anomalous events have created more headaches than answers for researchers who have attempted to find scientific validation for unusual UFO encounters. On the surface, some of the reported anomalies seem to be explainable using modern science. However, upon closer analysis, strange things tend to become even stranger.

Failure of car engines

The disruption of car motors, machinery, and electronic devices during a UFO event has been commonly reported. Thousands of these inexplicable stories have been duly recorded over the years and many volumes have been written in an attempt to understand the underlying principles involved.

Mark Rodeghier of the Center for UFO Studies analyzed 441 cases in which "the car, truck, or other motor vehicle in which a witness was either riding or in near proximity to, was seemingly affected by the presence of a UFO. Headlights, radios and even flashlights were also affected."

Of the vehicle failure cases summarized by Rodeghier, 10 percent noted an unusual phenomenon called "spontaneous engine restarts" at the end of a sighting. In reality, this figure is probably much higher considering the amount of underreported and underdocumented cases worldwide.

In these cases, the car's engine would mysteriously restart without the driver turning the key. One witness said: "As soon as the UFO flew away, the car, radio, headlights, switched back on by themselves. One second everything was completely dead, and the next, everything was running smoothly as if nothing had ever happened."

The witness said he was left with the feeling that his car had been stopped between the ticks of a clock: "Like time had completely vanished."

The Oz Effect

Another notable feature of many cases is the sudden unusual silence and an overwhelming feeling of isolation in the proximity of a UFO. Many people have noted that normal sounds – birds, insects, traffic – suddenly stop just before and during a close UFO sighting.

A man from Wisconsin reported that he had observed a UFO hovering over the treetops directly over his head once while deer hunting. He stated that the day had been windy and the trees were swaying and creaking pretty loudly in the breeze. What made him look up was the fact that all of a sudden the forest went "completely dead."

He noted that the trees had stopped moving as if "frozen in place." That is when he noticed a strange, dark, triangle-shaped object floating over the trees.

"It was a little bigger than a pickup truck and was solid black. J didn't see any lights or hear any kind of sound from it."

The hunter reported feeling like he was "looking up through a tunnel with me at the bottom and the UFO at the top. I knew that I was completely alone and that no one could help me."

As soon as the UFO passed overhead the forest returned to normal.

The experience of such unusual sensations around a UFO has been dubbed "the Oz Effect" by UFO researcher and author Jenny Randles and may indicate that there could be a field of influence that is being emitted around a UFO. Anyone close enough to a UFO would find himself completely contained within this field. The odd effects noticed by eyewitnesses could give us some kind of indication of the true nature of these energy fields. Unfortunately, anecdotal accounts of UFO experiences have rarely been followed up with rigorous studies of their content.

UFOs and time

Scientists brave (or foolhardy) enough to try and conduct proper research on the nature of UFOs have been unable to find satisfactory answers as to why UFOs seem to cause time distortions. Past interpretations of Einstein's physics leave little room for localized time anomalies, unless influenced by a gravitationally massive object such as a black hole.

However, the new kids on the physics block, quantum and string theories, may show that time and space are easier to influence than was previously thought. Some physicists believe that it is possible to engineer space-time itself and to surround a spaceship with a local space-time in such a way that locally, the light barrier remains intact, while from the outside the ship is moving at faster-than-light velocity. UFOs that seem to rapidly accelerate, change direction, or even disappear are actually operating conservatively from the viewpoint of their own internal time rates.

If someone or something came close enough to a ship that was creating its own space-time, normal time and space, as they know it, would cease to exist for them, and they would come under the influence of the artificial space-time.

This could explain some of the stranger aspects of UFO encounters, such as environmental sounds disappearing, isolation, the freezing of motors and electronic devices, and the feeling of time slowing down, stretching out, and losing all meaning. The UFO is literally creating an alteration in the local state of space-time, thus generating a major distortion effect that is experienced by the witness. Within this time anomaly the perceived forward motion of time could even disappear, allowing for the past, present, and future to intrude upon one another.

A glimpse of the past

In 1981, Linda Taylor and her mother were traveling by car to Chorlton, a district of Manchester, England. The normally busy road became strangely empty and the two women noticed a huge light in the sky that seemed to pace their car.

Linda told investigators that her car "jerked about" and slowed down despite her attempts to accelerate. Suddenly, an "old-fashioned" car appeared in the road ahead and drove straight toward the two women. At the same time the light in the sky turned into a metal disc that hovered over the main road.

As the UFO moved away from Taylor and her mother, the old car vanished instantly. When the women returned home they found that two hours were missing from their trip. As with some others who have had close UFO encounters, Linda later had several odd psychic experiences and further time lapses.

Time distortions may not always occur with a visible UFO nearby. In 1980, Peter Rojcewicz, now a professor of humanities and folklore at New York's Juilliard School, was in the University of Pennsylvania Library reading a UFO book suggested by another professor.

As he read, Rojcewicz noticed that someone was standing in front of him. Looking up, Rojcewicz saw a very gaunt, pale man, about six feet tall and weighing around 140 pounds. The strange man wore a black suit, black shoes, a black string tie, and a bright white shirt. His suit was loose, and it looked as though he had slept in it for days.

"He sat down like he had dropped from the ceiling – all in one movement – and folded his hands on top of a stack of books in front of him," Rojcewicz said. The man asked Rojcewicz what he was doing. Rojcewicz said he was reading about flying saucers.

"Have you seen a flying saucer?" the man asked. Rojcewicz said he hadn't.

"Do you believe in the reality of flying saucers?" Rojcewicz said he didn't know much about them and wasn't sure he was very interested in the phenomenon.

The man screamed: "Flying saucers are the most important fact of the century and you are not interested?"

The man then stood up, again, all in a single awkward movement, put his hand on Rojcewicz's shoulder, and said: "Go well on your purpose." With that, he left.

Rojcewicz was suddenly overwhelmed by fear: "I had a sense that this man was out of the ordinary and that idea frightened me. I got up and walked around the stacks toward where the reference librarians usually are. The librarians weren't there. There were no guards there – there was nobody else in the library…I was utterly alone and terrified."

The professor went back to the table where he had been reading "to get myself together. It took me about an hour. Then I got up and everything was back to normal; the people were all there."

It would seem that Rojcewicz could have been placed into a separate time-space field in order for his contact to occur. The entire episode may have occurred in the blink of an eye in normal time-space. But for Rojcewicz, an entire hour passed.

One gentleman, who reported his alleged UFO abduction on an Internet forum, said that when he was being returned from an abduction to the motel room where he was staying, he "noticed that there was a person in the parking lot below us (I and several 'Grays' were 'floating' in mid-air so I had a bird's eye view of the surroundings,) [who] seemed to be frozen in mid-step. Everything was dead quiet, and nothing was moving. It was as if time had stopped or frozen for the few moments it took for them to transport me from a UFO back to my room that was located on the second floor of the motel."

These interesting cases show that there is still a lot we have to learn from UFO reports. Investigators need to be willing to look beyond the traditional "by-the-book" questions and allow the witnesses to relate their entire experience – no matter how unusual it may be. Many researchers and databases fail to mention some of the stranger aspects of UFO encounters because they don't fit a particular belief system or bias. We can learn much more if researchers put aside their own personal feelings and allow the full information to come forward.

Currently, any theories and conclusions are really little more than speculation. Nevertheless, scientists who are not afraid to look beyond the norm are every day developing new concepts in physics and the true nature of reality.

Tim R. Swartz: Emmy Award-winning television producer and videographer. A photojournalist, Swartz has traveled the world investigating paranormal phenomena and other mysteries. He is also the author of popular books including The Lost Journals of Nikola Tesla *and is the writer and editor of the Internet newsletter* Conspiracy Journal.

FATE November 2005

Phone Call Out of Time

John Powell Riley

From 1955 to 1965 I lived in Geneva, Switzerland, with my charming Russian wife, Assia. She was warm and socially inclined by nature, so we did a lot of entertaining. When we weren't entertaining we were being entertained.

Among our friends was a small family of white Russians – that is to say, anti-Communist Russian refugees. Known to most members of the international colony in Geneva, the family included Tamara, Mara, her 25-year-old daughter, and Baboussia, the grandmother. Like many Russians, Mara was a brilliant linguist. She worked as a translator at the United Nations headquarters, and her income comfortably supported the family. She did simultaneous translations, the most difficult type, that very few are able to do. Mara could handle three or four languages, going from or to Russian, and her vocabulary in all of them was enormous. It had to include the special words and phrases of diplomacy, commerce, and several branches of science.

I marveled at this and wondered how a mind so crammed with all those words, and all that grammar, in so many languages, could still function normally in other respects and find the time and inclination for life as most of us know it. But Mara was exceptionally pretty and normal in every way, and she was as kind as she was beautiful. In short, she had character.

Eventually, my life changed, and I moved away from Geneva, losing contact with Mara. Fifteen years later, I was living alone on my 41-foot-sloop in Rochester, New York. Assia lived on the French Riviera. We were divorced but we remained close, then and now, and the embers of our love still smoldered. I phoned her every Sunday afternoon, and she phoned me once or twice during the week, sometimes just to say, "I kiss you, Johnny."

Assia always phoned at 4 AM my time, perhaps to keep the cost down, but more likely because she never took into account time differences in various parts of the world. I was not surprised, therefore, to be awakened by my phone one morning at that hour, and I knew it had to be Assia, although it was not a day on which she usually called; nobody else ever phoned me at 4 AM. I got out of my bunk in the aft cabin, put on my robe, and went into the main cabin to pick up the phone. By that time I was fully awake.

"Good morning, my little darling," I said.

Instantly I heard the sadness in her voice. "Oh Johnny, something terrible has just happened. Mara died." Assia was sobbing.

I was struck dumb for a moment. I pictured Mara as I last saw her – in perfect health.

Assia continued, "She had friends over for lunch and she choked on an olive pit. They didn't know what to do. She died before they could get help."

"Oh my God. How sad." It was all I could think of to say. "She had been married only a month. Another tragedy is that now poor Tamara and Baboussia will have nobody to support them."

Later that morning, when I went to my office feeling sad and depressed, I told my secretary about Mara. Mara the newlywed – the charming, kind, lovely young woman. Dead. Such a tragic accident. What is life all about? Why?

I had lunch with a friend and again Mara was the main topic of conversation. We spent the rest of our lunch time discussing life, trying to find reason in the scheme of things.

"One thing seems certain," I said, "we live in a world of consequences where the physical laws of the universe prevail without exception. Not even God rescinds them. You can be the best person in the world, but if I push you off a cliff, you will fall to your death and all your goodness will not save you. If you absentmindedly step in front of a speeding car, nothing in your character will have any bearing on the inevitable outcome."

My friend, who usually seized every opportunity to argue and play the devil's advocate, just nodded in agreement.

Over a period of about a year, whenever conversations turned philosophical, I never failed to mention Mara's death. I thought it the best example to illustrate the whims of fate that move us hither and thither "on a checkerboard of nights and days…then one by one back in the closet lays."

Assia and I, however, did not speak of Mara's death again. But many phone calls and about a year later, my phone rang again at 4 AM.

"Good morning, my little darling," I said.

"Oh Johnny, something terrible has happened. Mara died."

I was taken aback. "I know that, darling. She choked on an olive pit."

"How did you know that?"

"Why, you phoned and told me at least a year ago."

"Johnny, that is impossible," she said. "She died only yesterday."

FATE July 1995

REaLity SHIFtS

PMH Atwater

Perception determines "truth." We invent our own reality through our own perceptions and those of others, and by accepting what appears to be real as real.

History is filled with stories of people who, in "slipping between the cracks" of their own consciousness (thus altering how they perceived the world around them) uncovered different ways to experience reality. What they accomplished in doing this made an impact on society. You and I, all of us, have profited again and again because this happened.

Chester F. Carlson, for example, inventor of the Xerox duplication process and founder of the Xerox Corporation, was a devotee of a certain trance medium who channeled spirit beings. While attending a series of sessions with the woman, he eventually "received" the photocopy process from the spirit beings she contacted. After experimenting with the technique and making a few adjustments, the Xerox process was born, along with a multi-billion-dollar company.

George Washington Carver took the peanut, until then used as hog food, and the exotic and neglected sweet potato, and turned them into hundreds of products, including cosmetics, grease, printer's ink, coffee, and peanut butter. Carver said he got his answers by walking in the woods at four in the morning. "Nature is the greatest teacher and I learn from her best when others are asleep," he said. "In the still hours before sunrise, God tells me of the plans I am to fulfill."

How did George Washington Carver communicate with God during the wee hours of morning? He said it himself – through the assistance of angels and fairies. And he isn't the only one to make such a claim. Peter and Eileen Caddy and their colleague Dorothy Maclean give the same credits in describing the work they accomplished.

This troupe, along with the Caddys' three sons, took up residence near an inlet to the North Sea at Findhorn, Scotland, for the purpose of setting up a co-creative link between themselves and nature intelligences – that is to say, angels (what they later called "devas") and fairies ("nature spirits"). They became willing workers with nature's own in an attempt to co-create a garden the likes of which would defy every known rule of convention and climate. That was in 1962. Today, the Findhorn Gardens regularly draw people from across the globe to tour the premises and take classes at Cluny Hill College, classes on how to communicate with angelic forces and helper spirits while at the same time enhancing one's own sense of spirituality.

The people I have mentioned came to perceive reality from a vantage point other than the norm; then they used what they gained from that experience to benefit others.

Different ways of experiencing reality happen when individuals expand their consciousness. Whether accidental or on purpose, that shift in perception also alters the meaning and the importance of time and space.

Native runners expand reality

Documented cases of native runners, especially those in North and South America, illustrate this. In Peter Nabokov's book *Indian Running*, an anthropologist by the name of George Laird described what happened to one runner who lived in the southwestern part of the United States:

"One morning he left his friends at Cotton Wood Island in Nevada and said he was going to the mouth of the Gila River in southern

Arizona. He didn't want anyone else along, but when he was out of sight, the others began tracking him. Beyond the nearby dunes his stride changed. The tracks looked as if he had just been staggering along, taking giant steps, his feet touching the ground at long irregular intervals, leaving prints that became farther and farther apart and lighter and lighter in the sand. When they got to Fort Yuma, they learned that he had arrived at sunrise of the same day he had left them," thus arriving before he departed. The runner's altered perception enabled him to accomplish this feat; he did not allow himself to be bound by normal perceptions of time and space.

Let's not forget the Australian aborigines. Theirs is the oldest continually existing culture on Earth (around for at least 50,000 years), and they maintain an understanding of time and space – of reality – that deserves our attention.

What they call "dreaming" has little to do with sleep or dreams which occur during sleep. Dreaming for them is actually more akin to a type of "flow" where one *becomes* whatever is focused on and suddenly *knows* whatever needs to be known at the moment. Aborigines sometimes use drugs to achieve this state but, more often than not, drumming, chanting, rhythmic movements, and certain other sounds and rituals suffice. In this state of consciousness participants seem to "merge with" or "enter into" soil, rocks, animals, sky, or whatever else they focus on – including the "Inbetween" (what appears to exist between time and space, as if through a "crack" in creation).

These people believe reality consists of two space/time continua, not one – that which can be experienced during wake time and that during dream time, with dream time slightly ahead of its counterpart, yet capable of merging into all time, or what Pulitzer Prize-winning poet Gary Snyder calls "everywhen."

To Australian aborigines, wake time is where learning is acted out and utilized, but dream time is where learning is first acquired. For them, dream time is the place where all possibilities and all memory reside. Stories are told of aborigines who physically appear and disappear as they slip back and forth from one continuum to the other, from the here and now to the alternate universes they believe exist and the everywhen they know awaits them.

Wise ones, be they monks or shamans or healers or mystics, are like this. They know life extends beyond the boundaries of perception. Yet perception itself can be flawed.

Yes, it is a fact that individuals and societies have always organized the cosmos to fit their own preferred beliefs. This is what defines the relationship between heresy (independent thinking) and orthodoxy (mutually accepted bias). But it is also a fact that the bizarre can intrude upon one's life so dramatically that one is forced to shift one's awareness of real versus unreal.

Fiction can foretell reality

Reality shifts (sometimes called coincidences) take on many guises. Fiction, for example, sometimes foretells reality. Were the authors of prophetic works inspired by altered perceptions of reality?

The popular movie *China Syndrome*, starring Jane Fonda, depicted a nuclear facility meltdown. Three weeks after the movie opened, the same kind of disaster actually happened at Three Mile Island near Harrisburg, Pennsylvania.

The 1961 novel *Stranger in a Strange Land*, written by Robert A. Heinlein, told the story of a global chief executive who made decisions based on his wife's advice, advice she obtained from regular consultations with a San Francisco astrologer. In 1988, media headlines carried the story that Nancy Reagan frequently consulted a San Francisco astrologer, and that the advice she passed along to her husband Ronald Reagan, then President of the United States, was based on those consultations.

The novel *Futility*, an 1898 creation of Morgan Robertson, detailed the sinking of an unsinkable ship, the largest vessel afloat. This imaginary ship, named *Titan*, collided with an iceberg during April, resulting in a high loss of life because the ship carried too few lifeboats. Fourteen years later, with uncanny similarities, the real ship *Titanic* re-created what happened in the novel: The two ships had almost identical names; both ships were designated unsinkable; both were touted as the largest ships at sea; both collided with icebergs in April; both resulted in many deaths due to a shortage of lifeboats. Plus, both had strikingly similar floor plans and technical descriptions.

Radio broadcaster Paul Harvey aired a grim tale of three shipwrecked sailors and one cabin boy, adrift and facing starvation, who drew lots to see who would forfeit his life, so the others could survive. The contest was rigged to make certain the cabin boy, Richard Parker, lost.

Evidence used at the subsequent court trial that convicted all three of murder and cannibalism included a story written by Edgar Allen Poe. Titled "The Narrative of Arthur Gordon Pym of Nantucket," Poe's tale described three shipwrecked sailors who rigged a drawing of lots, then killed and ate their cabin boy companion, Richard Parker. Poe's story, which so accurately described the drama, every detail as it actually happened – including the victim's correct name – was written and published 46 years before the event happened, even before the participants were born.

The astonishing ability of fiction to accurately foreshadow what physically occurs happens more often than you might think. It's almost as if on some level, knowingly or unknowingly, consistently or occasionally, individuals can tap into or stumble across other dimensions of reality, as well as knowledge of a predestined or potential future.

Remarkable reality shifts also occur that cannot be correlated with any sort of imaginings:

Brad Steiger, in his book *The Reality Game and How to Win It*, tells about Charles W. Ingersoll of Cloquet, Minnesota, who appeared in a travelogue made and copyrighted by Castle Films in 1948. Ingersoll could be seen leaning over the rim of the Grand Canyon taking pictures with his 35mm camera. Yet Ingersoll did not go to the Grand Canyon in 1948. He had planned to do so, but his plans changed and his first trip there was made in 1955, when he took with him a newly purchased camera manufactured the same year of his trip.

A week after his return, he chanced upon the old travelogue in a store and bought it, discovering to his utter amazement that the film clearly showed him there in 1948 – holding a camera that did not exist until 1955. An investigation verified the incident and the dates, but no explanation was ever offered as to how Ingersoll could have appeared in a film showing him at a site seven years before he got there.

On October 21, 1987, Claude and Ellen Thorlin were sitting at breakfast. Ellen heard a disembodied voice ask her to tune in Channel 4 on their television set. Even though that channel did not receive broadcast transmissions in their area, Ellen turned the set on. There she saw the face of their dear friend and colleague, Friedrich Jurgenson, a well-known Swedish documentary filmmaker and the father of EVP (electronic voice communication with spirits). Ellen was shocked; Claude snapped a photo that recorded the image and the time – 1:22 PM. That time was 22 minutes into Jurgenson's funeral service that was occurring 420 miles away, a funeral service the Thorlins had been unable to attend.

When T. L. of Fort Worth, Texas, was 21 years old, he borrowed his parents' car for a drive from Darby, Montana, to Missoula, to visit friends. Staying later than expected, he found himself speeding back to Darby between one and two in the morning. At a place where the road wound around hills paralleling the river channel, the car headlights suddenly picked up a herd of 20 to 30 horses sauntering across the highway. With no time to hit his brakes and no place to pull off the road, T. L. hoped to avoid a collision by driving between the animals. Two large horses stopped directly in front of his path. The inevitable seemed his fate until, in the flash of an instant, T. L. found himself well beyond the herd, driving as if nothing unusual had happened. To this day he cannot explain how he missed hitting the horses. "It was as if I and my car were 'transported' to the other side of the herd," he said.

Each of these "coincidences" involved people as real as you and me, on days that began as ordinary days.

Changing our awareness

Are these events merely coincidences? Too much evidence from too many sources contradicts this idea. Something else is going on here.

The events described in this article underscored moments when subjective reality overlaid objective reality to determine experience. And when that happened, the future easily surfaced. This peculiarity occurred automatically, without provocation, and regardless of logic. What we call time – past, present, future – ceased to be sequential for these people and took on the aspect of simultaneity.

All of the cases – whether involving aboriginal or present-day societies, fictional or non-fictional themes – centered on men and women who encountered alternate versions of time and space. What occurred changed their perception of the world. It also changed their awareness of "future."

PMH Atwater: Internationally renowned researcher on near-death experiences and related phenomena. This article was adapted for FATE *from her book,* Future Memory: How Those Who See the Future Shed New Light on the Workings of the Human Mind (1996).

FATE May 1997

TIME TRAVEL MECHANICS

Time Travel and the Multiverse: Many Worlds, Many Timelines

Marie D. Jones and Larry Flaxman

Time travel has enchanted and intrigued us since the earliest days of fiction, when authors such as H. G. Wells, Samuel Madden, Charles Dickens, and Enrique Gaspar y Rimbau stretched and challenged our imaginations with images and tales of men and women who invented amazing machines and devices that could take them back in time or forward into the future. But because of the restrictions of light speed, and the paradoxes of going back to the past without damaging the future timeline, and a host of other obstacles and challenges, we, in fact, have remained stuck in the present.

Our scientific knowledge and technological achievement has yet to catch up to the limitless dreams of our imaginations. But just because we have yet to achieve time travel in our universe, in our particular point along the cosmic arrow of time, it doesn't mean it isn't achievable...and maybe the key is the universe itself. Are we limiting ourselves to our understanding only of the laws and possibilities of our universe, and leaving out of the equation other realities, other universes, with other laws and forces, paradoxes and limitations, possibilities and potentialities, far beyond our own?

In 2011, quantum physicists at the University of California at Santa Barbara, led by Andrew Cleland and John Martinis, designed a "quantum machine," as they call it, that might one day lead to proof of time travel and parallel universes. Their machine, a tiny little teleporter barely visible to the naked eye, involves making a tiny metal paddle cool to its ground state, the lowest energy state permissible by the laws of quantum mechanics, and then raising its energy slowly by a single quantum to produce a purely quantum state of motion. And, they even were able to put the device in both states at once, so it vibrated both slowly and quickly at the same time, in another sort of Schrodinger's Cat state of superposition. They posited that we can only see one of these potential states at once, and upon the act of observation, the state then splits into additional universes. Perhaps, there is a plethora of multiple or parallel universes all around us, but we cannot see them.

Wormholes

Wormholes could also be another possibility for teleportation, as physicist Max Tegmark suggested while attending a panel in January of 2008 at MIT to discuss the science behind the movie *Jumper,* starring Hayden Christiansen, about a man who can teleport all over the world at will. Tegmark was asked about the science behind the science fiction, and remarked that a wormhole was one possible way of getting something quickly across space-time. However, after admitting that wormholes do appear to be theoretically possible, Tegmark commented that the actual trip would be rather grueling because of the instability of the wormhole. "It could collapse into a black hole, which would be kind of a bummer."

Many scientists look to the possible existence of other levels of reality, or other universes, as a way to make time travel work outside of the restrictions of light speed and paradoxes. Imagine another universe alongside our own where the laws of physics are so completely different that what is impossible here is mundane and trivial there. Multiple worlds, even, where each is different from the other, or perhaps an infinite number of universes where many would be exactly like our own.

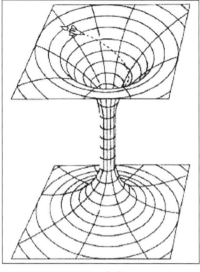

Wormhole

Hey, you might even exist in some of them just the way you are right now. In others, you might be rich, famous, handsome or even a cockroach! In fact, perhaps you might even be invisible in one of them!

But we are getting away with ourselves here, and when the talk turns to the multiverse and other similar concepts, it's easy to start dreaming of science fiction worlds with every possible kind of life and all sorts of amazing machines and devices…and time travelers passing effortlessly back and forth between the past, present and future as if it were nothing more than a visit to a few Saturday morning garage sales.

Parallel universes

Parallel universes have long been a mainstay of science fiction films and stories. Parallel universes can exist individually, or grouped together as the "multiverse," and offer the possibility of a totally different reality in which someone, or something, can exist, or hop back and forth between. The laws of nature may be different in one parallel universe as they are in another, and in respect to time travel, would provide multiple versions of the future in which someone could exist, or not exist at all. Light speed

Rod Taylor as Herbert George Wells, the Time Traveller,
in the 1960 film The Time Machine

limitations may not exist in a parallel universe, and the paradoxes that keep us from traveling back in time would be null and void if we could jump into a different historical timeline.

Two great fictional examples of a parallel universe would be *Alice's Adventures in Wonderland,* written by English author Charles Lutwidge Dodgson under the pseudonym Lewis Carroll, and C.S. Lewis's *The Chronicles of Narnia.* Both involve some sort of portal or wormhole, such as a rabbit hole or a large piece of furniture, through which a person can enter into another realm.

Theoretically, parallel universes may be the result of a single random quantum event that branches off into an alternative universe. This is the "Many Worlds Interpretation" or MWI, of quantum mechanics, originally formulated by physicist Hugh Everett in 1957, and posits that each time a different choice is made at the quantum scale, a universe arises to accommodate that choice, thus creating infinite new worlds popping up all the time. These new worlds are being constantly created and could cause problems for a potential time traveler.

Physicist David Deutsch wrote in "Quantum mechanics near closed time-like lines" for the 1991 *Physical Review,* that if time travel to the past were indeed possible, the many worlds scenario would result in a time traveler ending up in a different branch of history than the one he departed from. Deutsch, of Oxford University, is a highly respected proponent of quantum theory, and suggests quantum theory does not forbid time travel, but rather sidesteps it, referring to the traveler's ability to go into another universe, a parallel universe, and avoid the paradox limitations.

Deutsch's idea of parallel universes, the multiverse, or "shadow universes," was described in his interview with *The Guardian* (UK) in June of 2010 ("David Deutsch's Multiverse Carries Us Beyond the Realm of Imagination") as being "coincident with, somehow contiguous with, and weakly interacting with, this one. It is a composite, a layer cake, a palimpsest of universes very similar but not quite identical to each other." The number of these shadow universes could be enormous, and Deutsch points to photon experiments that suggest possibly a trillion of them or more. He also suggests that future-directed time travel will essentially only require efficient rockets and is on the "moderately distant but confidently foreseeable technological horizon." When it comes to past travel, the multiverse might save a time traveler from the pesky grandfather paradox. He uses an example of a writer who wants to go back in time with a copy of Shakespeare's *Complete Works* and help the bard complete *Hamlet*. It can happen, but in the multiverse view, "the traveler has not come from the future of that copy of Shakespeare."

Many-Minds Interpretation

Another offshoot of the MWI is the Many-Minds Interpretation, which extends the MWI by positing that the branching off of worlds occurs in the mind of the individual observer, was introduced in 1995 by theoretical physicist H. Dieter Zeh, Professor Emeritus of the University of Heidelberg and the discoverer of decoherence. The Many-Minds Interpretation was widely criticized and somewhat ignored, mainly because of issues involving the theory that the mind can supervene on the physical as the mind has its own "trans-temporal identity." The mind may select one identity as its own non-random "reality," yet the universe as a whole remains unaffected, which presents additional problems when dealing with different observers ending up with the same measured

The time travel machine in Dr. Who

realities. The actual process by which the mind of the observer would select the single, measured state is not explained by the MMI.

Alternate timelines, each with their own forward arrow of time and their own history, may exist then, allowing time travelers to jump into another version of history and override those pesky paradoxes. Imagine being able to jump into a time line where you do get your dream of marrying your high school sweetheart, but, finding out she's an evil tramp as soon as you say, "I do," you could jump back into your original historical timeline, where you didn't marry her and instead ended up three years later marrying her sister, your true soul mate, and living happily ever after.

Noted theoretical physicist Michio Kaku, author of *Parallel Worlds and Hyperspace,* writes in his book, *Physics of the Impossible: A Scientific Exploration Into the World of Phasers, Force Fields, Teleportation and Time Travel,* of three ways around the paradoxes of time travel.

The first is that you simply repeat past history and fulfill the past, and that everything you do once you are back in time was meant to happen anyway, a sort of destiny. This opinion is also mirrored in the views of famed physicist and superstring theory proponent Brian Greene, author of *The Fabric of the Cosmos: Space, Time and the Texture of Reality and The Elegant Universe: Superstrings, Hidden Dimensions and the Quest for the Ultimate Theory.* Greene writes that outside of the quantum world, in the classical science of the grander scale, we exist static and unchanging at various locations in what he calls the "space-time loaf" of the block we call space-time. These moments are unchangeable and fixed. Using a wormhole, if one were to indeed go back in time to a certain point, or date, one would find that there is only one version of that date, and that your presence back in time would simply be a part of the original version of that moment. That moment has one incarnation, though. "By passing through the wormhole today and going back to that earlier time you would be fulfilling your ironclad destiny to appear at that earlier moment." He points to the wormhole time machine itself as the culprit, with one opening or the other passing through time more slowly than the other end, but each opening is still going forward in time. Thus, there will also be a limit as to how far back in time you could travel in the first place.

The second of Kaku's paths around the paradoxes involves having some free will to change the past, but within limits, so that you could go back and try to kill your grandfather, but something would prevent you from doing so. The gun might lock up, or you might drop it and shoot your foot instead and end up in the hospital. No matter what, you would somehow be prevented from knocking off your grandpappy.

The third involves the universe splitting into two universes to accommodate the time traveler. His example offers someone going back in time to kill their parents, and in one timeline the people look like your parents but are different because you exist in a different timeline.

The many worlds approach could solve all the paradoxes in two ways. If we imagine the timeline of our universe as a line drawn on a board, then we can draw another line to represent the universe that branches off from the first.

When you go back into the river of time, the river forks into two rivers, and one timeline becomes two timelines, and so on, and so on. Say you planned to kill your own father. You go back in time and you do the dirty deed. If the river of time does indeed have many forks, this would not be a problem. "You've just killed somebody else's father. In that timeline, you don't exist, but you exist because you jumped the stream," Kaku writes.

This idea would also solve another thorn in the side of physicists when discussing time travel: the radiation effects of entering a wormhole, which would no doubt destroy any time traveler, and also end up in a loop, the feedback of which would become so strong it would destroy the wormhole. "If the radiation goes into the time machine, and is sent into the past, it then enters a new universe; it cannot reenter the time machine again, and again, and again." Kaku points out that the main problems involving time travel and wormholes specifically center on the issues of the physics of the event horizon, as in the stability of the wormhole, the deadly radiation and the wormhole closing once it was entered. Solve those issues and real time travel might be a piece of cake!

Well, not a piece of cake, but all physicists agree that once they come up with a Theory of Everything that unites the four universal forces of electromagnetism, gravity and the strong and weak nuclear forces and formulate a complete theory of gravity and space-time, then time travel might be as close as finding a wormhole big enough, stable enough and open enough to get a time machine through. Not to mention the sheer amount of energy necessary to do this, which might require harnessing the power and energy of a neutron star, or finding that elusive exotic matter scientists are looking for, or a good source of negative energy, and we are far from doing any of these things.

Oh, then there is the problem of creating the machine. And let's not forget finding or creating a wormhole that could handle it! An interesting problem was brought up by physicist and cosmologist Paul Davies, author of *About Time: Einstein's Unfinished Revolution* and other books. In an interview with Discovery.com called "Is Time Travel Possible?" he discusses wormholes as time machines and potential time travel tourists from the future, but with the caveat that "theoretically, it would take more than 100 years to create a 100-year time difference between the two ends of a wormhole, so there's no way that our descendants could come back and tell us we're wrong about this." So, it's all about timing, then…pun intended.

The multiverse is the most widely mentioned theoretical "time travel paradox killer," because it involves more than just one parallel universe, thus allowing for an increasingly possible world where the laws of physics are just right for time travel. If we can get from here to there, that is.

There may be a massive number of other universes out there, possibly even an infinite number, or maybe just 20 or 70. While our astronomical observations cannot at this time detect them, it is most definitely a theoretical possibility that many cosmologists and physicists are considering. These universes may or may not be like ours. In fact, they may or may not even have the same laws of physics or distribution of matter, or even number of spatial and temporal dimensions. Some will undoubtedly be "dead" and others will have life forms that we cannot recognize or even imagine. Others still may have duplicates of us living their own separate lives and timelines. Maybe Big Bangs are going on constantly, 24/7/365, all the while creating new universes.

The multiverse theory is not new, especially for readers of science fiction and fantasy, where other worlds beyond ours is a given. The actual term was coined in the year 1895 by psychologist and philosopher William James and is now a mainstay of theoretical and quantum physics, as well as a part of our religious beliefs, mythological stories, and spiritual/New Age thought. The multiverse has been equated with everything from the kingdom of heaven of the Judeo-Christian Bible to the akashic field or hall of records or various planes of existence of more metaphysical and spiritual thought, to the multiple timelines and dimensions of more paranormal and anomalous concepts.

Cosmologist Max Tegmark took the multiverse theory to the next level by creating a classification level for potential other worlds:

- LEVEL ONE: Domains beyond our cosmological horizon – the least controversial type, what lies beyond the vantage point, yet likely has the same laws/constants, just with possibly different initial conditions than our own.

- LEVEL TWO: Universes with different physical laws/constants and other post inflation bubbles. Far more diverse than Level Ones, these bubbles also vary in initial conditions as well as other seemingly immutable aspects of nature.

- LEVEL THREE: Quantum universes/Many Worlds Interpretation – may exist alongside us on the quantum level where the random quantum processes cause the universe to branch into multiple copies, one copy for each possible outcome.

- LEVEL FOUR: Ultimate Ensemble – Other mathematical structures, where *all* potential alternate realities can exist. Anything and everything are possible in terms of location, cosmological properties, quantum states, and physical laws and constants. These exist outside of space-time.

Each level of multiverse has its own characteristics that separate it from the other levels, and for our purposes, the focus for time travel would be on those we humans could exist in, and possibly travel between. One of the ways Tegmark himself differentiated the levels was by stating that in Level One, our doppelgängers could live somewhere else in three-dimensional space, but in Level Three they would live on another quantum branch in an infinite-dimensional Hilbert space, yet as the Many Worlds Interpretation states, likely would not be able to interact once the split into another branch occurs. Those found in Level Two might be like "bubble universes" that have different physical laws and constants, and each new bubble is created by splits that occur when spontaneous symmetry breaks occur in Level Three.

Tegmark describes these levels in detail in his book *Universe or Multiverse*, and states that the key question isn't so much whether there is a multiverse, but rather how many levels it has. He admits that nature may have tricked us into thinking that our vantage point was the extent of reality, a fixed view of the world around us. "Einstein taught us that space is not merely a boring static void, but a dynamic entity that can stretch (the expanding universe), vibrate (gravitational waves), and curve (gravity)."

Many scientists refer to the multiverse as more of a "pocket universe" concept, indicating different regions in space-time that are unobservable, but still a part of our one universe. Inflationary cosmology does state that these pocket universes can be self-contained, with different laws of physics, different particles and forces and possibly even different dimensions.

Even the popular string theory allows for potentially trillions of possible universes, each one compatible with relativity and quantum theory. Michio Kaku states in *Physics of the Impossible* that, "Normally communication between these universes is impossible. The atoms of our body are like flies trapped on flypaper. We can move freely about in three dimensions along our membrane universe, but we cannot leap off the universe into hyperspace, because we are glued onto our universe." Gravity, however, can freely float into the spaces between universes. Kaku also points to one theory where dark matter, which is an invisible form of matter surrounding our galaxy, might actually be "normal" matter in another universe.

But the question remains, can we travel back and forth between these different worlds with different laws and arrows of time? Again, theoretically, it would require a shortcut through space and time...like a wormhole...and a means of safely getting through that wormhole should it be stable and traversable. So even though the multiverse theory takes care of some of the paradoxes by offering up alternate timelines and histories in which one can both go back to the past and kill their grandfather (while not killing him at the same time), it appears as though there is still no realistic way of actually doing that.

The multiverse also allows for alternate futures as well, and for multiple, alternate versions of "you" to exist in any number of historical timelines with different outcomes depending on the choices you make in each baby bubble universe. In an article titled "Riddles of the Multiverse" for PBS.org's August 2011 *Nova* series, University of Southern California professor of physics and astronomy Clifford Johnson was asked straight out about whether or not the multiverse could ever be "visited" by humans. His response was that we must first work out the physics of these other universes, in order to determine when and whether it makes sense to "cross over from one to the other." He did admit that it is possible that the stuff we are made of, the matter and forces that make us and hold us together, may not allow us to ever leave our four-dimensional universe and go to another. Imagine doing so and, well, coming undone!

So for now, it seems, we just don't yet have the brainpower and technology to leap and jump between worlds, to cross timelines and experience as many pasts, presents and futures as we would like. That knowledge and technology may exist, though...out there...somewhere in time.

Reprinted in FATE, with permission of the publisher, from *This Book is from the Future: A Journey Through Portals, Relativity, Wormholes*

FATE May-June 2013

InterView With Michio Kaku

Phyllis Galde

(FATE editor Phyllis Galde had the distinction of a personal interview with renowned physicist Michio Kaku, author of Physics of the Impossible: A Scientific Exploration into the World of Phasers, Force Fields, Teleportation, and Time Travel. *Kaku is the Henry Semat Professor of Theoretical Physics at the City University of New York Graduate Center.)*

Other dimensions

Galde: You are a proponent of string theory, which envisages an 11-or 13-fold dimensional universe. How do you envisage these extra dimensions?

Kaku: We live in a three-dimensional world. Length, width, height, and we also have the fourth dimension, which is time. But anyone who talks about higher dimensions is sometimes called a crackpot. Now, when I was a child, I used to go to the Japanese tea garden in San Francisco where there are fish swimming in a shallow pond. I imagined being a fish myself. And if I was a fish, I could travel forward, backward, left, and right, but the concept of 'up' made no sense because the pond is the universe.

So, I imagined there was a scientist there who would say, "Bah, humbug. There are no other dimensions other than forward, backward, left, and right. There's no such thing as up. What you see is what is. If you cannot measure it, it doesn't exist." Then I imagined as a child reaching down and grabbing the fish, lifting the scientist into the world of up, hyperspace, the third dimension. What would he see?

He would see a world where beings move without fins, a new law of physics. Beings breathing without water, a new law of biology. Then I would put the fish back into the pond, and what stories he would tell. A universe beyond the universe.

Well, today many physicists believe that we are the fish. We spend all our lives in three dimensions, going forward, backward, left and right, up and down. Anyone who talks about another, unseen dimension is considered a crackpot. Well, not anymore. This summer [2009], the largest machine that science ever built, the Large Hadron Collider, 27 miles in circumference, costing eight billion euros (about 10 billion dollars), will be turned on. And we hope to get evidence of the eleventh dimension. One of time, 10 of space.

We work in an area called string theory, which used to be a bunch of outcasts in the physics community. But now, we're center stage. We have gotten the major faculty positions at Harvard, Princeton, Yale; all the young crowd coming up are string theorists. My generation suffered enormously because people thought, "Oh my god, this is *Star Trek*, beam me up to the higher dimensions."

The young people, however, have the benefits of realizing that we are now the center of gravity. What happened? What happened was we physicists began to smash atoms, and we have a pretty good understanding of the theory of particles. It's called the Standard Model. Except it is the ugliest theory known to science. Why should Mother Nature at a fundamental level create this ugly theory called the standard model? It has 36 quarks, it has eight gluons, it has three W bosons, it has a whole bunch of electrons, a whole bunch of neutrons, it just goes on and on and on.

Why should this be nature's supreme theory? It's like getting an aardvark, a platypus and a whale, start shaping them together and calling this nature's finest evolutionary creation, the byproduct of millions of years of evolution of the earth. I would like to believe that these 36

May-June 2009
$5.95
www.fatemag.com

FATE

True Reports of the Strange and Unknown

Crop Circles Revealed

Physicist
of the
Impossible

Michio Kaku

quarks, eight gluons, three W bosons, are nothing but the lowest octave of a vibrating string.

Now, these strings are special. They are not ordinary strings. These strings, when they vibrate, create the musical notes which correspond to the particles we see in the universe. We can explain why we have leptons, muons, hadrons, photons, neutrinos, the zoo of subatomic particles; it's nothing but the lowest vibration of the string. The normal aspect of the string is that they only vibrate in 10 or 11 dimensions. They vibrate in 10 dimensions. When you add membranes or beach balls, they can vibrate in 11 dimensions. So we think that's what the Big Bang was. The Big Bang was an instability in 11-dimensional hyperspace.

Einstein wanted to read the mind of God. That was his goal in life. He wanted an equation one-inch long that would allow him to read God's thoughts. That's what dominated his thinking. For the first time now, we have a candidate for the mind of God. The mind of God is cosmic music resonating through 11-dimensional hyperspace. That is, we think, the mind of God.

Galde: So you think Einstein was right?

Kaku: He was on to it. He didn't go far enough, basically.

Flatland

Galde: Could the unseen dimensions contain or conceal various paranormal phenomena such as UFOs, ghosts, psychokinesis, metal-bending?

Kaku: Well, a hundred years ago, at the turn of the last century, the idea of these higher dimensions began to penetrate British society. People began to speculate about these things. And then people began to ask a simple question: If you look down on a lower-dimensional world, how would they look at you?

People began to realize that if you look down on a flatland, people living on a tabletop, you would have the power of a god. You'd be able to walk through walls. You'd be able to disappear, reappear. You'd be able to reach inside a safe, steal the gold without ever breaking open the safe.

If you were to put a flatlander in jail – what is jail? Jail is a circle. You draw a circle around one of these cookie men, flat as a pancake on a tabletop. A circle is prison. So, you say to these people, "Why don't you escape prison?" And they say, "Why? How? Everywhere I move I bump into the wall." And then you say, "Well, why not move up?" And then they say, "There is no such thing as up. Only mystics and crazy people talk about up. There's no such thing as up."

Well, if you were to just lift them off, what would they see? As they float in three dimensions, they would see cross-sections of our world as they begin to float vertically upward. So, if they were to see us, what would we look like? If they looked at my chest, they would see three balls. They would see two arms and a torso. Three balls. As they move higher and higher, the three balls coalesce into one. So that's my neck. And as they go higher, the balls disappear entirely, and that's because they're over my head. That's how they would visualize us. They would think of us as a god because we could break out of jail, we could go right over walls, nothing can stop us.

Around 1900 in Victorian England, they began to ask: "Who lives in these higher dimensions? Who has the ability of walking through walls, disappearing, reappearing somewhere else, reaching into a safe, grabbing the gold." And they said, "Ghosts have that power."

Around the turn of the 20th century there was a whole movement saying that ghosts could live in these higher dimensions. The Church got involved; they said that maybe God lives in the fourth dimension. One theologian even said that four dimensions are too small for God. God should live in infinite dimensional hyperspace.

Well, nothing happened, because you couldn't measure these dimensions. You couldn't do anything with it. There was no theory of these higher dimensions.

Then Einstein comes along and says that time is the fourth dimension, and the simplest consequence of it is: the atomic bomb. That scared the hell out of people. So, for a generation all of this thinking was lost. People said: "Oh my god, the fourth dimension means like the sorcerer's apprentice, opening up powers, cosmic powers, that we were not destined to see; that is nuclear energy, the power of the sun coming from $E=mc^2$."

Parallel universes

Kaku: We string theorists, a hundred years later, are beginning to reexamine things and realize that perhaps there *are* these higher dimensions. We are going to try to measure these dimensions: (a) with the Large Hadron Collider, and also (b) through dark matter. We now realize that there is an invisible form of matter called dark matter. It makes up 23 percent of the universe. It's invisible, but it has weight. We hope to find evidence of dark matter which is predicted by string theory.

Also, we want to have direct evidence of a parallel universe. If a parallel universe exists in this room, then Newton's laws would be wrong in this room. The inverse square law, for example, only works in three dimensions. If the universe is four-dimensional, it would be the universe cubed.

At the University of Colorado, they've actually done the first experiment measuring gravity on a small scale to test Newton's theory of gravity. We use this theory of gravity for our spaceships and our space probes, but not inside a room. Well, the experiment was done a few years ago and the result came out negative. But to me that simply means there's no parallel universe in Colorado. There could be parallel universes everywhere, but in Colorado we find no evidence of that.

This is a very hot topic. It is now a legitimate subject to look for evidence of parallel universes and higher dimensions.

ESP in the lab

Galde: What about psychic people who can see into other dimensions? I am 180 degrees different from you. One of my brothers is a nuclear physicist, and so he has this kind of brain. I am very intuitive. I grew up in a haunted house seeing ghosts and otherworldly creatures. I have all my life.

Kaku: Well, I'm a physicist. We only believe in what we can measure with reproducible results. Dark matter we can measure. It is invisible; it makes up a huge chunk of the universe. It's mysterious, but we know it's there. Higher dimensions, we're not sure. Remember we're building the Large Hadron Collider, we're building these experiments on dark matter. We can't say one way or the other. We think it is true. That's why we're devoting our lives and our professional careers to building machines which may access some of these higher dimensions, but we can't say one way or another.

Galde: Have you ever had any otherworldly experience yourself?

Kaku: Well, Richard Feynman, who was one of the founders of modern physics – he won the Nobel prize – put himself in a hyperbaric chamber. He tried to see whether he could leave his body. And he did. And he wrote about it. There is a rather famous essay where he writes about being put into this chamber with sensory deprivation and then seeing himself rise from the chamber and then look at himself from a distance.

The question is, what does that mean? He said that he's not sure what it means but it is compatible with dreaming. He's not saying this is dreaming, but the body can imagine itself leaving itself. That doesn't mean it actually happened; it means the body can imagine itself doing that.

As a physicist, I work on what is measurable, what is testable, what is reproducible in the laboratory. These experiments are going on now, so this is serious business.

Let's talk about telepathy and psychokinesis. We physicists approach the concept of telepathy and psychokinesis in terms of what we can demonstrate in the laboratory. We now know that with an MRI scan we can begin to read the thoughts, primitive thoughts, that are racing inside our minds.

In Japan, for example, you can show somebody a picture of a dog, a cat, a table, a ball. Read their MRI scans. Have a dictionary between the scan and a ball, the scan and a dog, and tell every time what you are looking at. With the MRI machine, you can "read the thoughts," simple thoughts, of somebody looking at simple objects. Maybe 10 objects. But in the future, we should be able to exponentially grow that number. We should be able to tell whether or not somebody is thinking about a chair, a table, a dog, a house, a rocket ship, or what have you, because we have the brain patterns listed.

Also, if you put a chip in the brain we can then begin to have the brain control objects around it. This is a very primitive form of psychokinesis.

A stroke victim at Brown University has been placed into a device connecting his partially dead brain to a laptop. He can control the cursor on the screen. He can now do crossword puzzles, he can surf the web, read email, write email, and he's paralyzed.

What was once forbidden, accessing people's thoughts, the secrets are now slowly coming out.

93

Extraterrestrial contact

Galde: Do you think there is a chance for mind control if we have such chips in our brains, if we have implants?

Kaku: So far the answer is no, because all we do is read what already exists. If you want to have somebody think of a ball without showing them a ball, we don't know how to project that into that person's mind.

If we ever encounter extraterrestrial civilizations, they may be at a point where they can access the human brain without having to use language. But we are only children doing this.

Galde: To travel the huge distances which separate the stars and the galaxies, one must travel at speeds in excess of light or else make use of black holes or postulated "wormholes" in space-time, or journey times will be in thousands or millions of years. Is such interstellar travel a realistic possibility for advanced civilizations, or are such things always to remain in the realm of science fiction?

Kaku: First of all, if you talk to the average scientist about UFOs, aliens, intergalactic travel, and stuff like that, most of the time their eyes roll up to the ceiling and they start to giggle. This is called the giggle factor. They say the distances between stars are so great that UFOs, interstellar travel is not possible.

But that's using today's physics. Today it is impossible for us to go to the stars. It's impossible for us even to go much beyond Jupiter. But that assumes today's technology. If you assume a civilization is a thousand years, a million years, more advanced than us, then whole new realms of physics open up. A million years, on the scale of the universe, is nothing. It's just the blink of an eye. So, I don't laugh. I don't giggle when people talk about extraterrestrial civilizations because maybe they're there and we're too stupid to know it.

If you had a galactic civilization, how would they explore the universe? They would not send Captain Kirk going from planet to planet to planet. That is the stupidest possible way to explore the galaxy. There are billions of planets out there. You can't send a starship going to every single planet. What you do is get a robot that replicates itself, lands on a moon (moons are quite stable), digs the soil, and makes copies of itself; millions of copies. They shoot out to other moons, create copies of themselves, and they shoot out. Starting with one robot, you get a million. Then a million times a million. Then a million times a million times a million. And pretty soon you have a sphere expanding at the speed of light containing trillions upon trillions of these probes, probing the galaxy.

Now where have we seen that before? That's a virus. The virus is the simplest way for one molecule to colonize your body to give you a cold in two weeks. One molecule infects trillions of cells to give you a cold.

A galactic civilization would land on our moon and build a probe to build copies of itself. Now where have we seen that before? The movie *2001: A Space Odyssey*...the most realistic encounter with extraterrestrial intelligence.

Stanley Kubrick, when he made the film, interviewed astrophysicists and had 10 minutes of the film with interviews, and they laid it out: This is the most mathematically efficient way to explore the universe. Then he cut the first 10 minutes of his own film. And then this film became very mystical. But if you watch it, it is the most realistic encounter with a civilization in outer space.

Galde: Do you think something like HAL could happen? Where the computer gets intelligent and it starts controlling things?

Kaku: I think *2001* was off by a hundred years. It should have been *2100*. In 2100 we'll have an operating moon base. Right now, we're so primitive that if there is evidence of visitation, we would never know. Let's say that on our moon right now there is a probe that is a million years old, left by a passing galactic civilization that has used our moon as a base to explore this sector of the galaxy. Would we know it? No, we are so primitive, we wouldn't even know it.

Then the other question. Carl Sagan asked himself this question: Are we advanced enough to know that our sector of the galaxy is inhabited? Let's say that there is a galactic civilization, and many of these planets are inhabited. Would we know? And the answer is "no."

Let's say that we're walking down a country road and we see an anthill. Do you go down to the ants and say, "I bring you trinkets, I bring you beads. I give you nuclear energy. I give you ant paradise, ant utopia.

95

Take me to your leader"? Is that what you tell them? Or do you have this urge to step on a few of them? If somebody's building a 10-lane super-highway next to an anthill, would the ants know what a 10-lane super-highway was? Would they be able to communicate with the workers? Would they even know that these are humans who are building this thing? They'd be clueless, totally clueless. They wouldn't know how to communicate. They wouldn't know the frequencies, they wouldn't know what a 10-lane super-highway was. They don't know what a car is, they don't know what a truck is.

The distance between ants and us is actually quite small compared to the distance between us and what is called a type-three civilization. So if there is a type-three civilization in our back yard, we wouldn't even know. They could be right there. Ants just staring at a highway, wondering, what is this?

Time travel

Galde: Do you believe it's possible to make a time machine?

Kaku: It may be possible. It seems to be consistent with the laws of physics. You need fabulous amounts of energy, comparable to a black hole. Michael J. Fox with his DeLorean cannot do it.

Einstein said that time is a river, a meandering river. We measure that with our satellites. A GPS satellite slows down in outer space. We measure that every day. Your GPS would fail without Einstein. But the new wrinkle is, the river of time may have forks. If the river of time forks, then perhaps you can go backward in time without a time paradox.

So, you go backward in time and meet your teenage mother before you are born and she falls in love with you; you're in deep trouble. But if you hop stream, if the universe opens up a parallel universe, then you've basically met somebody else's teenage mother who looks like your teenaged mother but is not. There are no time paradoxes involved.

These are solutions of Einstein's equations. This is not just somebody dreaming a science fiction story. We have mathematical realizations of all these things. Many, many designs have been proposed, all of them consistent with Einstein. The problem is energy. You need fabulous amounts of energy to do this.

It takes a lot of energy to keep me on the floor. It takes the earth just to keep me on the floor. So, it would take a star to bend the fabric of space and time. And that's what you need to create a time machine. Anyway, in my book I give a design.

Galde: Do you ever read science fiction?

Kaku: Yes, I used to read the Asimov series.

Galde: I taught science fiction in high school. You've read *A Wrinkle in Time*, by Madeleine L'Engle?

Kaku: Right. In fact, in that book, it was a tesseract that was the gateway. A tesseract is a four-dimensional unraveled hypercube.

That one percent

Galde: Are there any UFO researchers' arguments you find compelling?

Kaku: I get a lot of sightings, but 99 percent of them can be dismissed as radar echoes, swamp gas, the planet Venus, weather satellites, meteorites, atmospheric anomalies…it's that one percent that gives you the willies. It's that one percent that is multiple sightings by multiple modes. They are the hardest to debunk, the famous one being the JAL sightings where you had an object off a JAL airline.

The hardest to dismiss are those that involve radar sightings, visual sightings, by not just one person but a whole crew on an airplane.

What we need…see, this will go on forever. Forever and ever people will say, "I saw something." And then people will say, "Well, what did you see?" What we need is more direct, tangible proof. That is, alien DNA. If we had alien DNA that would end it right there. But so far, no alien DNA.

Second of all, an alien ship. That would also end it. Any sign that there's an alien culture, information that is different from our information. That would end it right there. But some people say, maybe our technology came from aliens. Well, it's not a testable theory.

Galde: Reverse engineering?

Kaku: It's not testable. I can say that it's not reverse engineering because I know the people who developed this transistor or that thing, and it was done by hard work and patience, not by mind reading. But when you talk about visitation, you need hard proof. That requires either alien DNA or an alien ship. Until that happens, this is going to go on forever. People will argue forever, whether that was a meteor or a flying saucer.

Galde: Some say that the aliens can cloak themselves.

Kaku: Well, we're going to be able to cloak ourselves very soon. We will be able to cloak an object under visible light in a few decades. It's in my book. I have a whole chapter on invisibility. Maybe they're here. Maybe they are invisible. We would never know.

But my personal attitude is that we may not be very interesting to them. They may come and visit us once in a while, but would you engage in a conversation with ants? You may not.

We think we're so great that they're going to want to come down and give us all the fruits of their technology. Why would they do that? We're not that interesting to them. If they can go from star to star, they are automatically 2,000 years ahead of us, meaning that we may not be that interesting to them.

Phyllis Galde: Owner, publisher and editor of FATE; *owner and publisher of Galde Press.*

FATE May/June 2009

THE EVIDENCE FOR TIME TRAVEL

J. H. Brennan

Schoolteacher Jane O'Neill had a lifelong interest in architecture and history. That's why she visited Fotheringhay Church in 1973. Fotheringhay, in Northamptonshire, England, was the place where Mary Queen of Scots was executed. It was the sort of building that drew her like a magnet.

The visit seemed normal enough. She spent a good deal of time admiring a splendid picture of the crucifixion behind the altar and an arch that held a dove. The bird's wings followed the curve of the arch.

Some hours later she mentioned these items to her friend Shirley, who had visited the church many times. Shirley looked at Jane blankly. She'd never seen the crucifixion picture nor the arch. Jane rang the local postmistress, who arranged flowers in the church every Sunday. The postmistress told her there was no arch and no picture of the crucifixion.

A year later, Jane went back to Fotheringhay Church. The outside was exactly as she remembered it, but when she went inside she knew at once she was in a different building. It was much smaller, and there was no painting of the crucifixion. Even the dove behind the altar was totally different from the one she'd seen.

Thoroughly disturbed, she got in touch with a local historian. What he told her was staggering. The Fotheringhay Church she had visited matched in every way the description of a building that had been pulled down in 1553. Jane O'Neill seemed to have traveled back in time!

O'Neill is not the only one to have experienced a time slip. Biologist Ivan Sanderson walked briefly into 15th-century Paris while on a remote road in Haiti. He thought he was hallucinating until his wife, who was with him, confirmed that she was seeing the same thing. Historian Arnold Toynbee was the victim of temporal slippage not once but five times – and he wrote his classic *Study of History* as a result.

But while these people – and many others like them – certainly felt they'd entered another time, can we trust their judgment? Is time travel possible?

Newtonian physics, the foundation of most of our practical technology, doesn't tell us how to travel through time, but it doesn't say time travel is impossible either. In Newtonian math, time can flow backward or forward without influencing the outcome of the equations.

Relativity Theory, on the other hand, clearly shows there are circumstances in which time travel can – indeed must – occur.

Einstein spelled out one set in his famous Twins Paradox. In the Twins Paradox, one twin joins the crew of a spaceship capable of traveling close to the speed of light. The astronaut takes off into outer space, while his twin stays home.

Assume both twins were 30 years old when the astronaut left, and the space voyage lasts five Earth years. On the ship, the astronaut twin ages five years according to every measure he can apply. So, by the time he gets home again, he's 35 years old.

But if the spaceship is traveling at 99 percent the speed of light, the Theory of Relativity shows that time is moving seven times slower on board than it is on the ground. That means the twin who stayed home has aged 35 years – and when his astronaut twin returns to Earth, the earthbound brother would be 65 years old.

In other words, just because the astronaut raced at breakneck speed around the galaxy, he's now 30 years younger than his twin brother.

Fotheringhay Church, Northamptonshire

Or put another way, he has voyaged 30 years into the future so far as life on Earth is concerned. And that, by any reasonable criterion, is time travel.

But it's time travel in one direction only, from the present to the future.

Tipler's time machine

Albert Einstein announced his Special Theory of Relativity in 1905. Sixty-nine years later, a University of Maryland physicist named Frank Tipler used its insights in plans for a working time machine. He published his ideas in *Physical Review*, under the bewildering title "Rotating Cylinders and the Possibility of Global Causality Violation." It turned out that a "global causality violation" was as weird a piece of geometry as you're ever likely to come across: a path that winds through space and turns around in time.

Tipler's idea was to create a closed time-like line (as the peculiar path is called) by building a machine that distorted both space and time.

He was even able to explain how to do it in a single sentence: "Relativity suggests that if we construct a sufficiently large rotating cylinder, we create a time machine."

The sort of cylinder needed would have to be very large indeed – too big to build on Earth. Initial calculations showed it would be too long to lay across the whole east-west sweep of the United States. It would also have to be heavy – far heavier than lead, for example, or any other substance used in our current technology. What was needed was a super-dense material, that has enormous mass but takes up very little room. Tipler pointed out that this sort of matter actually exists – in neutron stars.

Neutron stars are stars that collapse under their own weight, but don't go all the way to becoming a black hole. The electrons inside their atoms are plunged into the nucleus where they fuse with protons to become neutrons (hence the name). The atoms themselves are fused together so that the whole star becomes one great atomic nucleus. It's the densest substance in the universe. If you could extract enough to fill a teaspoon, it would weigh more than one billion tons.

But even at that weight, a teaspoonful would not be enough to create a Tipler Cylinder. Physicist Fred Alan Wolf has estimated that the cylinder would need to be about 40 kilometers across and more than 4,000 kilometers long. For that, you would need about 100 neutron stars.

It's clear that a Tipler Cylinder is far beyond our present capability. But that's not to say that building a Tipler Cylinder is impossible. Most scientists agree that if something is theoretically possible, technology will learn how to do it sooner or later.

In the case of the Tipler Cylinder, some form of advanced technology would be used to push a hundred neutron stars together. To work, the cylinder needs to have a spin of about 10,000 revolutions per second. Fortunately, most neutron stars revolve at that speed anyway. Put them together and you have a cylinder that, on its surface, is spinning at about three quarters the speed of light.

A twist of time and space

Once the cylinder was in place, space and time would begin to distort – in clearly defined zones. Immediately surrounding the cylinder would be a 20-kilometer-wide zone where the fabric of space and time is changed in an almost unimaginable way. Physicists call this the "Deadly Zone."

There's no way you could exist in such a zone. In fact, you probably couldn't get into it in the first place – you would be repelled by the very nature of space and time at its boundary.

Surrounding the Deadly Zone is the Zone of Time Reversal. This is the area of space in which time runs backward. Get yourself into that zone and you're a time traveler.

The time travel zone is surrounded by a Null Time Zone where time stands still. This zone is surrounded by a Positive Time Zone – where time runs in the familiar past-to-future direction.

Since Einstein published his relativity theories, many physicists have speculated that black holes or wormholes of the type made famous in *Star Trek* might form time gates. But if so, everybody agrees they would be strictly one-way. The exciting thing about Tipler's time machine is that, in the words of one of his colleagues, "It is possible, starting from any point in the outer regions of space, to travel to the interior, move backward in time…then return to the original position." In other words, a Tipler Cylinder would allow a time traveler to make a return trip.

But there is something about Frank Tipler's machine that is more exciting still. We know we can't build a Tipler Cylinder today – but if humanity builds one in 1,000 years, or 10,000 years, or even a billion years' time, the gates it will open will extend throughout the entire space-time continuum.

That means if a Tipler Cylinder is ever built, by humanity or even an alien race, at any time in the future, then its time gates actually exist today. Somewhere in space, beyond the solar system, our own astronauts may soon find a zone of time reversal.

Don't be a litterbug

This is interesting speculation, but is there any evidence that a Tipler Cylinder will actually be constructed in our future? The answer seems to be a resounding yes.

The first piece of evidence is circumstantial. Each year in the United States and throughout the world, there are thousands of reported sightings of disc-shaped objects in our skies. Many believe they are craft from an alien planet, and perhaps they are. But isn't it an odd coincidence that the gravitational stresses surrounding a Tipler Cylinder mean the safest type of ship to enter the time zones is disc-shaped?

Even if UFOs are not flown by time travelers, there is evidence across the globe that we have had visitors from a distant future. Time tourists have left litter.

Somebody once dropped several hundred metal balls in South Africa – 2,800 million years ago, long before anybody manufactured metal balls.

The same goes for a wide range of anomalous items: the polished concrete block wall found in the depths of an Oklahoma coal mine and estimated to be 286 million years old, the delicate gold chain of similar vintage found in Illinois, the carved stone found in Iowa that was dropped some 260 million years before humanity evolved on the planet, and a decorated metal vase from Massachusetts more than 600 million years old.

There is a limited number of explanations for finds of this type. One obvious possibility is that they are simply misdated. But it's difficult to see how a scientist could misdate something like the Massachusetts vase that was discovered encased in rock.

Another possibility is that the artifacts were dropped not by human time travelers, but by visitors from space. Most scientists agree that life must exist elsewhere in the universe and some of it must be intelligent. Some experts suggest there may be as many as 10 million advanced civilizations in the Milky Way galaxy alone.

But many scientists are generally united in the opinion that however much intelligence there is out there, it hasn't visited the Earth. This is largely based on calculations showing that the amount of energy required for interstellar travel is literally astronomical.

Even if the scientists are wrong on this, many of the temporally misplaced artifacts are of undoubted human origin. The carved stone from Iowa, for example, featured multiple representations of an old man's face. There was a fossilized human shoe print found in Utah shale some 500 million years old. A human footprint was discovered in the Turkmen Republic of Eastern Europe, next to that of a three-toed dinosaur.

The dinosaurs disappeared from our planet, quite suddenly, 65 million years ago. Until that happened, the most advanced mammal on the face of the globe was a little tree-dweller no larger than a mouse. Humanity itself is supposed to have evolved in Africa no longer than

100,000 years ago – and while there may be a case for adjusting this date backward, nobody suggests we could have walked the Earth in the days of the dinosaurs.

Unless, of course, we traveled back in time to do so.

J. H. Brennan: Author of Time Travel: A New Perspective (1997).

FATE February 1997

Russians Design and Test Time Machines

Paul Stonehill

Russian scientists have been experimenting with a machine that can physically alter time for anything inside it. Vadim Alexandrovich Chernobrov, who sent me the materials I used for writing this article, and his colleagues have created a time machine that, although still limited, has enormous potential – and enormous dangers.

Chernobrov graduated from the Moscow Aviation Institute, where he studied at the Department of Astronautics and Automatic Flying Craft. His degree work and research thesis involved a project dealing with a promising space transport system (containing an unusual electromagnetic engine) that can be transformed into a time machine. Besides his main work at the Moscow Aviation Institute, Chernobrov is also a science editor and a columnist for several editorial offices of Russian newspapers, including *Rossiyskiye Novosti*, a major Russian newspaper. He is also an engineer responsible for designing space craft, and since 1988 he has labored to create a UFO-like flying craft.

The time machine the Russians created is currently limited. It can only slow down or speed up time by four minutes in a 24-hour period. Chernobrov hopes that in the future the machine will be able to move through time and space at much faster speeds. Because of many years spent on research, the Russian scientist is ever more certain that a part – but only a part – of all UFOs are vehicles for travel through time. He believes that in all probability they have arrived here from the future.

Chernobrov mentions Albert Einstein's alleged secret calculations for the US Navy experiments in 1943 (the so-called Philadelphia Experiment). The Russians believe that Einstein destroyed his manuscripts because he was afraid his ideas about time travel could be used to harm humanity. The Russians (including Chernobrov) are certain that Einstein's manuscripts contained mathematical substantiation that it is possible to travel to other dimensions and through time. There are also rumors of an electromagnetic field that the US military allegedly used (based on Einstein's design) to create an invisible ship.

Methods to alter time

What method did Chernobrov use to alter time? He knew that neither chemical reactions, nor revolving flywheels, nor gravitational vortices were very promising. All these processes have a very limited effect on time. It is also almost impossible to control these processes. Therefore, Chernobrov rejected them in his attempt to create transport systems.

Instead, Chernobrov's theory explains time (a physical phenomenon) under certain conditions, as a manifestation of electromagnetic forces. It follows that with the help of such forces time could be influenced. A machine based on such theory can be easily controlled and may be able to provide higher performance.

The first model of the time machine was named *Lovondatr*. It began functioning on April 8, 1988. The results were modest. The machine was created with volunteer aid from experts from the Moscow Aviation Institute, the Khrunichev aerospace plant (this entity is now heavily involved in joint projects with American aerospace companies that work for the US defense industry), and scientific design bureaus Salyut and Energiya.

From 1988 to 1993 four experimental time machines were created. All were lentil-shaped machines. They were constructed around a closed space that has special electromagnetic properties. Each also has a control

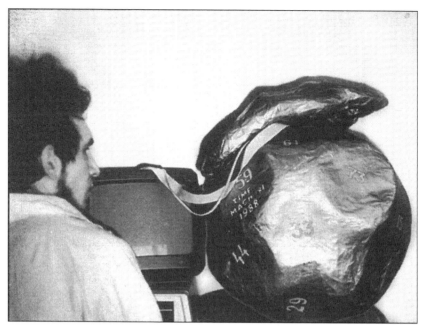

Russian engineer Vadim Chernobrov and his time machine

unit, a power unit, and instrumentation. The needed electromagnetic fields configuration is created by a series of electromagnetic operating surfaces nested in each other under the *matryoshka* principle. (*Matryoshka*s are the Russian wooden dolls in peasant dresses that have successively smaller dolls fitted inside them.) These layers of flat electromagnets were twisted into an ellipsoidal shape. The outer layer was either attached to the power shell or was itself a power source. The operating conditions, specified by the control unit, could be diversified, and for each model of time machine it was possible to choose the most optimum frequency, tension, and switching mode ratios. When Chernobrov was designing his promising space transport system based on time machine technology, he concluded that the most optimal shape for it would be the shape of a flying saucer.

The maximum value of the altered time was established inside the smallest *matryoshka*. During experiments scientists observed (as was expected) altered time outside the apparatus, too. Time measurements were taken with a pair of quartz generators and a standard clock, and precise time signal readings were duplicated by electronic and mechanical clocks placed in the payload section. The first time machine had a difference in readings of up to one-half second an hour, while subsequent, modified machines showed a time difference of up to 40 seconds an hour.

The volume of payload in the center of the time machine was about the volume of a soccer ball. Therefore, dogs, the traditional pioneer travelers, were not used. The honor belonged to mice. The first experiments, which transported insects and mice into the past, killed the experimental animals, despite the time difference being only two seconds. Those humans who were not careful and stood too close to the time machine during the experiment developed symptoms of disease, analogous to ones developed by American sailors who participated in the Philadelphia Experiment. After the layout of the machine was improved, the animal test pilots survived the process of transporting them through time. Chernobrov believes that humans will be able to travel through time by the beginning of the next century.

The first experiments with the time machine have slightly raised the curtain that shrouds the mystery of time. According to the preliminary data, time has many measures: It is heterogeneous and changeable. The present is but a passage of the multi-varied future (the crown of the tree) into the mono-varied past (the tree trunk). Travel into the future is possible only through one branch, but the return to the present is possible through any of the branches, because they will all return the time machine to the primordial point.

Travel into the past guarantees that the time machine will come to any event that has occurred. And if the visit does not result in undesirable contacts and the movement of history is not altered, the return to the starting line should not be hindered. Otherwise, the return will take place through another branch. But the movement of history will change only for the time travelers: They will not be able to get to the point from which they started and will find themselves in another version of the present – that is, in a parallel world.

A deadly superweapon

Chernobrov understands what drove Albert Einstein to destroy his manuscripts. In a world where there are wars, a time machine can be turned into a superweapon. Here is an example: We know that the force of destruction of any explosive depends on the velocity of percussion. If we place the charge into the capsule where time flows differently, then we can create a high explosive bomb from a simple grenade. What if we use an atomic bomb instead of a grenade? A time machine is a superb means of transportation – it is elusive, and no aircraft, no rocket can compare with it.

Chernobrov is certain that although Einstein burned his manuscripts, the ideas that the great scientist developed could not be burned away. No direction in science can be blocked. What Chernobrov is concerned about is making sure that evil does not come from such ideas. He has closely watched the work of other specialists who want to open the mystery of time. These experts have approached the problem from many directions but were not walking the right path. Not long ago Chernobrov found alarming reports about scientific research into certain high temperature semiconductors (no true time machine could be created without them). Then, these reports stopped appearing in the international press, as if the scientists had been silenced. Chernobrov thinks the answer lies with the military. The military has made this subject classified.

This alarms the Russian scientist, because of the time machine's potential to become a terrible superweapon. Chernobrov calls upon all experts involved in the development of time machines to participate in international, peaceful cooperation.

But perhaps Chernobrov should look no farther than his own back yard. The Russian newspaper *Trud* published a report in its July 30, 1992, issue about a flying saucer-like aircraft that underwent successful test flights. The craft was created and built at a military-industrial facility by experts from the experimental mechanical engineering design bureau. The apparatus's movement is based on the following principle: A high temperature superconductor travels about and is exposed to the rapid flow electrons. The report in *Trud* tells us that the Russian military has come close to creating a time machine of its own. It means that the creation of a real, usable time machine is not far off.

Paul Stonehill: Researcher of Russian paranormal and UFO phenomena; frequent FATE contributor.

FATE April 1996

TIME TRAVELERS ARE AMONG US!

Dr. Bruce Goldberg

Time travelers are among us! My abductee patients have been telling me this under hypnosis for years. Scientists and others with similar biases view such reports as "hypnotic hearsay," but I now have firsthand evidence.

For years I've had to rely on the accounts of my patients to learn about these time travelers, or chrononauts. But recently I began using a travel exercise to visit the fifth dimension (hyperspace) and have experienced contact with our future visitors myself. (In fact, I have modified the Southern Californian "have your people contact my people" to "have your time traveler contact my time traveler.")

The first chrononaut I met was named Traksa. He lives on Earth in the 36th century, when time travel will be achieved through teleportation. As a result, he can beam his physical body back or forward in time through an enlarged wormhole – a portal in space caused by a black hole.

Chrononauts travel back in time to monitor and exert influence on our lives. Before I made contact with Traksa, several of my time-traveler abductees informed me that their chrononauts knew exactly who I was and had been monitoring my work for years.

Traksa has been using me to get the message out concerning time travel and spiritual growth. It was he who guided me into discovering future-life progression, age progression (going into the future of this life), superconscious mind taps, conscious dying techniques, and so on. My media interviews have also been influenced by Traksa.

Despite their influence, however, time travelers do not usurp our free will. We can always reject their counsel, as I ignored Traksa's telepathic guidance concerning my ET abductee work for two decades. The chrononauts must be a patient breed to have waited out my stubbornness. After working with abductees for more than 20 years, I finally took Traksa's advice and went public with my findings in 1997.

A detective tracks a time traveler

Chrononauts intervene in the past to stimulate our intellectual growth. Traksa told me a story about one of his visits to our time a few years ago. He traveled in Chicago dressed in civilian clothes (time travelers normally wear white robes) to attend a meeting of scientific researchers. His mission was to telepathically guide their research.

Following the conference Traksa returned to the fifth dimension. His sudden dematerialization was observed by a private investigator on his lunch break. Realizing he had left a folder behind, Traksa rematerialized to the same location and was witnessed again by the private eye.

Aware that he was being observed, Traksa played along. He led the detective to a coffee shop, where he ordered a sandwich and a cup of coffee. After he left, the private eye bribed the waitress, wrapped Traksa's coffee cup in a handkerchief, and ran a check on his fingerprints with the FBI and Interpol.

Those attempts were futile, of course. After all, how are we going to identify a man who won't exist for 1,600 years? These little mind games are one method by which chrononauts stimulate our intellectual growth.

To a similar end, chrononauts have sent objects back in time for us to discover in order to make us question our view of our own history:

- In 1844, a gold thread embedded in a stone eight feet beneath the ground was found. It originated from 320 to 360 million years ago.

- A metallic vase with beautiful inlaid figures, found in Dorchester, Massachusetts, is about 600 million years old.

- A chalk ball found 246 feet below the ground in Laon, France, in 1861 is 45 to 55 million years old.

- In 1871 a coin-like object was discovered in a well near Lawn Ridge, Illinois. It is between 200,000 and 400,000 years old. The coin is nearly circular in shape with crude figures and unintelligible inscriptions on both sides. Records show the first such coins were made in Asia Minor during the 8th century BCE.

- A clay figurine found in Nampa, Idaho, in 1889 seems to be about two million years old.

- A partial sole from a shoe was uncovered in Nevada in 1922. This item is 213 to 248 million years old.

- Hundreds of perfect metal spheres found in South Africa bear three parallel grooves around their equators. These limonite iron ore samples, which do not occur naturally, cannot be scratched with a steel point. They date back to 2.8 billion years ago, when the only life on this planet consisted of single-cell organisms.

A brief history of time travel

Time travel will be discovered around 3050 by a man named Taatos. He is the Hermes of ancient Egypt and the very first chrononaut. Prior to transporting himself back in time, Taatos sent holographic images into the past. These were the source of many oracular visions described by ancient civilizations such as the Egyptians, Greeks and Romans.

Time travelers communicate with us during our dream cycle. It is here, in REM (rapid eye movement) sleep, that we leave our physical bodies and enter hyperspace, gaining the ability to see fifth-dimensional people, including chrononauts.

This explains the importance of the "sleep temples" of the ancients and their dream incubation techniques. In Egypt, for example,

115

certain priests were trained to translate the dreams of the ill into a cure. These priests were called "Masters of the Secret Things" or "Scribes of the Double House." They administered potions to afflicted individuals to promote dreaming.

The wormhole mechanism that Traksa uses to visit our time will be perfected during the 35th century.

Monitoring and abductions by time travelers have increased markedly during the last 500 years. Traksa has told me that there are many time travelers around today. They come from 1,000 to 3,000 years in the future. They do not hold public office or place themselves in positions of attention. They remain in the background, observing us from the fifth dimension in order to remain undetected.

Normally we can only see in three dimensions: length, width and depth. We cannot see time (the fourth dimension of the space-time continuum), nor anything beyond time (the fifth through the twenty-sixth dimensions). For chrononauts to interact physically on Earth, they must slow their vibrational frequency and enter our three-dimensional world. That's the only time we can see them in our waking state.

As extradimensional beings, chrononauts have abilities that help them in their mission. They can communicate with us in our dreams, place us in suspended animation, and levitate us at will. The have mastered hyperspace travel between dimensions, can move through walls and solid objects, and float through the air. Though some less advanced chrononauts sometimes make errors, they learn to manipulate time and space with proficiency. The chrononauts are also adept at genetic engineering. By changing our chromosomes, they have increased the rate of human evolution. It's hard for some to understand what motivates this interference. To what end do these visitors play games with detectives, bury things in our past and fiddle with our genes?

Chrononauts are spiritual people. They follow us from lifetime to lifetime, tracing our souls back to previous lives and monitoring our spiritual unfolding. Their ultimate purpose is to facilitate the perfection of the human soul to allow for ascension and the end of the karmic cycle. There are also future problems – wars, pollution, infertility – in this and parallel universes that they are trying to avert by assisting us now in our spiritual progress.

As we grow spiritually, so do they. They are us in the future.

116

Interpreting an experience

Dear Dr. Goldberg,

I was pulling out of a parking lot onto a very busy three-lane street. Suddenly I realized that the pavement under my car was solid ice. I slammed on the brakes but couldn't stop. I just slid into the street and into the oncoming traffic.

I looked to my left and there was a red car bearing down on me at about 50 miles per hour. There was no way it could avoid hitting me. In seconds I should have been directly in front of it. So I closed my eyes, put my head down, and waited for the crash.

When nothing happened, I looked up and saw the red car to my right. It was stopped at the intersection down the block. Despite the heavy traffic on the street, there were no other cars closing in on me. I was able to get my car under control and drive away.

This event may not sound strange to you, but believe me, it was not physically possible for this to have happened. There was no way for the car to go around me, yet there it was on the other side of my car. Can you explain this? – *G. Carlson, Arlington Heights, Illinois*

Goldberg: Your story has three possible explanations. First, you may have actually experienced the teleportation of your car and the others. Another possibility is intervention by an angelic being, or spirit guide. The third possibility is that a time traveler from the future may have interceded on your behalf. These chrononauts often function as spirit guides while in the fifth dimension.

Dr. Bruce Goldberg has degrees in dentistry and counseling psychology. He is the author of Time Travelers from Our Future: An Explanation of Alien Abduction *(1998).*

FATE February 1999

LOST IN TIME AND SPACE

Nonpeople from Nowhere

Scott Corrales

The concept of parallel universes – worlds somehow superimposed over our own – is not new. It has normally been relegated to the realm of the fantastic: the madcap world on the other side of the looking glass in *Alice in Wonderland*, the fanciful realm of Narnia in *The Lion, the Witch and the Wardrobe*, or the many supercharged, high-adventure parallel realms that can be found in science fiction and heroic fantasy. From a literary standpoint, the creation of a parallel universe allows the author to explore possibilities that cannot be found in our own linear reality.

Therefore, we find artistic works in which the protagonists encounter their "doubles," worlds in which the outcome of a war ended differently than in the protagonists' prime reality, or completely different levels of existence ranging from the heavenly to the horrific.

These authors would perhaps be surprised – even dismayed – to learn that truth is stranger than fiction (to abuse the hackneyed expression), and that reality offers stories no less strange than the product of their imaginations.

Beyond the circles of the world

In the 5th century BCE, Anaxagoras, a Greek philosopher of the Ionian School, posited a theory by which he hoped to explain the origin of all things, a daunting task even from antiquity's perception of reality. Anaxagoras stated that matter had originally existed as atoms, thus paving the way for the philosopher Democritus' own atomic theory. While only fragments of this Greek genius's work survive to our times, some of them are of great interest.

Anaxagoras believed that "other men and other living species" lived in a sort of anti-Earth, bathed in the light of a sun and moon, and whose inhabitants "like ourselves, possess cities and build clever objects." The philosopher placed his anti-Earth on what we might wittily call the "flip side" of his flat, discoidal earth.

The surviving fragments of his treatise, *On Nature*, do not tell us if Anaxagoras believed that there could be contact between the sentient beings of both worlds, but another group of thinkers thousands of miles away had developed a similar cosmology and made it part of their religion.

The *Puranas*, a summary of Hindu mythology, philosophy and ritual, speak of the *dwipas* as part of their cosmological beliefs. These levels of existence, for want of a better description, consist of seven continents – Jambu, Plaksha, Shalmali, Kusha, Krauncha, Shaka, and Pushkara – with their respective oceans, mountain ranges, and inhabitants.

It is hard to separate the clearly metaphorical, such as the oceans of "sugarcane juice and clarified butter" that surround some of these metaphysical lands, from those which are more firmly grounded in reality. Some of the provinces into which the Jambu *dwipa* is subdivided, for example, appear to correspond to the physical subcontinent of India, bordered by the Himadri Mountains (Himalayas) on the north and the Salt Water Ocean (Indian) on the south. Beyond these confines, the rest seem to merge into the unreality we have come to associate in the West with mythical lands like Lyonnesse, Tir na Og, the Isle of Avalon, and St. Brendan's Isle.

The concept of the *dwipas* became known in the West during the late 19th century through the work of the Theosophical Society, fueled by the general interest in Eastern matters that characterized that period of history.

Strange people in other-dimensional lands

"It is the opinion of many at the present day," states Charles Johnson, F.T.S., in the April 1889 issue of *The Path*, "that the almost grotesque myths and fantastic geographical and astronomical descriptions contained in the religious writings…are really deliberately contrived and constructed allegories by which the ancient sages sought to veil…the sacred truths which could only be declared in the secret recesses of the temples."

In the 1960s, French scientist-turned-occultist Jacques Bergier took an interest in the metaphysical Hindu realms, believing that there could be some truth to them according to the principles of modern mathematics. Bergier noted that "Riemman surfaces" are composed by a given number of layers that are neither on top of each other nor beneath one another – the layers simply coexist. Bergier was almost certainly simplifying matters for the layman reader, but the mathematical conclusion was that space could be far more complex than it initially appeared to be.

"If Earth is one of these [Riemman] surfaces," writes Bergier, "fantastic though it may seem, it is possible that there are unknown regions which are normally inaccessible and do not appear in a map or globe of the world, but which nonetheless exist indeed. We did not suspect their existence any more than we suspected the existence of germs, or the invisible radiation of the spectrum, prior to their discovery." (*Visa Pour Une Autre Terre de Jacques Bergier,* Albin Michel, 1974).

Did the iconoclastic Bergier find a way of justifying the beliefs of both Anaxagoras and the Hindu scribes who composed the *Puranas*? Are there indeed "spaces within our space" that developed separately from our own, perhaps accessible only through what we might term dimensional doorways, wrinkles in space/time, and other descriptions? As unlikely as the possibility may appear, it would account for the widespread belief in worldwide folklore that there are places which humans can enter and never leave, or which can only be entered, Brigadoon-style, at certain times of the year or every so many years. Could the phantom cities often visible in the Arctic (such as Alaska's Muir Glacier) be mirages – not of our own cities, but of those cities whose inhabitants "build clever objects," as Anaxagoras said long ago?

The Man from Tuared

But we aren't done with Bergier just yet. In 1954, in the wake of violent protests in Japan, which was then just emerging from the "proconsulship" of General McArthur, Japanese authorities believed that the riots were being instigated by foreign agitators and mandated that the passports of foreign visitors to the country at that time be scrutinized for irregularities – telltale signs of forgery by terrorists or antigovernment forces. Bergier tells us that officials came across a guest at a Tokyo hotel whose papers seemed to be in order, but there was a slight problem: The government issuing the passport did not exist.

The document showed no signs of having been tampered with. The bearer's photograph was clear, as were the fingerprints. Yet Japanese officials were at a loss to find a Republic of Tuared anywhere in their atlases, despite the bearer's strident protests that his country occupied most of the Sahara Desert, stretching from Mauritania on the west to the Sudan on the East. True, the man had come to Japan on a shadowy mission – to purchase weapons to aid in emancipating all Arab countries from foreign oppression.

According to Bergier, the nameless Tuaredian hastily summoned a press conference to make his case, and the press corps tried in vain to find his country, even after entreaties to the United Nations and the Arab League. The man from Tuared was committed to a Japanese psychiatric hospital, where he presumably remains to this day – a stranger in a strange land.

Granted, the entire event could have been a hoax – an effort by some Saharan nationalists at establishing their own country and deceiving customs officials. Certainly, a similar situation could have occurred only a few years ago, when the Puerto Rican Independence Party started issuing its own "Republic of Puerto Rico" passports for those who wished to renounce their US citizenship. According to the party sources, the passports issued by the nonexistent republic were accepted by customs officials in a number of foreign countries. Nonetheless, could some strange phenomenon have deposited a citizen of a major North African country from another *dwipa* within our own world?

Something similar had occurred a century earlier and thousands of miles away. In 1850, a man was found stumbling in a daze down the cobbled streets of a German village. When authorities brought him in for questioning, he stated that his name was Josef Vorin, "a citizen of Laxaria in Sakria." German officials tore their hair out trying to find these places to no avail. Herr Vorin's fate is also unknown.

In the 1970s, renowned Spanish UFO researcher Antonio Ribera looked into a possible "intrusion" of a nonexistent world into our own. But rather than involving a republic with dark designs on its own world or this one, it concerned a small archipelago in the Pacific Ocean.

Under the Southern Cross

The coordinates couldn't have been more specific: 47.9°S, 118.15°W. And if the information was correct, somewhere in the immensity of the Pacific was a group of islands that no one could seem to find, but whose government was busy issuing postage stamps.

It all started when Antonio Ribera received a call from a fellow researcher, an enthusiast of Antarctica and all of its outlying islands, asking him if he had ever heard of an archipelago known as the "Hesperides Islands."

Ribera's friend died shortly after raising the question. His heirs provided the ufologist with all of their father's notes and information regarding the Hesperides. It was thus that Ribera momentarily put aside his UFO inquiries to chase after this improbable archipelago located at the coordinates mentioned earlier.

In order to spare the reader a trip to the atlas, be assured that a scan of a number of atlases shows nothing except deep blue sea at the coordinates in question. The nearest land masses are Easter Island and Juan Fernandez. Yet among the papers given to Ribera was a curious booklet entitled *A Study of the Hesperides Islands*, written in English by one John Callender and published in Great Britain in 1962. The 20-page booklet included some interesting maps with geographic features identified in Spanish and French along with some photographs of the remote islands. The booklet's prologue suggested that the islands were unknown to the point "that they were no longer depicted in the immense majority of maps and cartographical works."

Unlike an island depicted on a child's pirate treasure map, we have hard "facts" on the Hesperides: The archipelago consists of Great Hesperides, Lake Island, and the islet of Rap, followed by five atolls covering a total surface area of 100 square kilometers. The geographic features on the larger islands are well marked: Mt. Franklin, the Merced River, and a large lake at the center of "Lake Island" in a mixture of English, Spanish, and Polynesian names. Their location makes them a sort of antipodean paradise, watered by brief rain showers and basking in a temperate climate. The vegetation is characteristic of the Polynesian islands, and its volcanic geology reveals the presence of basalt, rhyolite, trachyte, and other minerals.

According to the papers inherited by Ribera, the islands were discovered in 1850 by "a Scottish whaler named McNall" and claimed as his personal property. Even more intriguing was a memorandum to the Spanish Naval Command stating that the archipelago had been purchased by a Madrid-based syndicate. At this point we begin to fall down the proverbial rabbit's hole that leads us to places like Bergier's Tuared.

Apparently, the Madrid-based syndicate had also rechristened the Hesperides as the "Dougherty Islands," and had further proclaimed an "independent state" whose application for membership in the United Nations was rejected. Colonel Antonio Baeza, the original compiler of the information, formally requested that the Spanish Navy send an expedition to the Dougherties and seize them, but his request was turned down. The Navy was understandably unwilling to waste fuel to reach an empty patch of ocean.

The government of the Dougherty/Hesperides Islands issued interesting postage stamps in Esperanto and drafted a constitution in the same language. Ribera notes that more than a constitution, the document is a formal Instrument of Occupation of the islands by the "Stato Hespero" (State of the Hesperides, in Esperanto), dated June 15, 1965, and declaring the "total occupation of the Dougherty and Hesperides Archipelago with the intent to capture, colonize, and establish a presence, and thereby establish a new state to be known as the Confederation of the Dougherty and Hesperides Islands." Signatories to this instrument were one Dr. Denewakara, one General Mayer, and one Professor Bellavini.

As if things weren't odd enough, the Dougherties had a national anthem ("Under the Southern Cross"), a capital in the village of Starpol, and ministries of the interior, treasury and culture.

The three rectangular postage stamps issued by this nonexistent republic commemorated freedom of religion, space travel and the rights of mankind. The stamps came in denominations of 50 and 75 unknown monetary units.

Taking a deep breath, Antonio Ribera launched his investigation. One of his colleagues, the late Andreas Faber-Kaiser, secured highly detailed maps of the South Pacific from NORAD, showing beyond any doubt that there was little beyond great quantities of saltwater to be found at 47.9°S, 118.15°W. Another researcher, Jose Luis Barcelo, managed to connect with the shadowy "Madrid-based syndicate" and confirmed its existence, but not its connection to the Dougherties. Having reached a dead end, Ribera set the matter aside.

At this point, a number of rational explanations parade before us: the creation of a bogus tax haven for European millionaires and billionaires; a fictional target created for a military exercise, similar to the nonexistent countries used in US Army and Navy war games; an intelligence exercise conducted by Spain's CESID for its own inscrutable purposes; or simply an elaborate fiction similar to our modern role-playing games, but on a grand scale.

On the other hand, could the phantom archipelago be a real bone of contention between the great powers of another world that coexists within our own, and from which information and living beings sometimes leak out? Perhaps the man from Tuared, still locked up in his padded cell in Tokyo, can tell us all we need to know about these islands.

Rogues' gallery

Scores of books dealing with the subject of mysterious disappearances have been written over the past five decades. Some of these are concerned with disappearances in our planet's oceans (such as the so-called Bermuda Triangle and Japan's Devil's Triangle), others deal with human disappearances near geographic features such as Vermont's Mt. Glastonbury, Puerto Rico's El Yunque, and Africa's Mt. Inyangani, while still others retell the stories – mostly apocryphal – of 19th-century characters disappearing from street corners and empty fields.

If we are willing to admit that humans and animals often do disappear in a way that baffles our best police investigators, we must also be willing to accept the possibility of people appearing out of nowhere under equally baffling circumstances. But in order to narrow the focus of this article, the monstrous entities that often appear out of thin air (the Mothman, the Chupacabras, Bigfoot, etc.) will be excluded. One does not even wish to imagine the kind of *dwipa* they must hail from.

These strange citizens from elsewhere, like the man from Tuared, may have no idea that they have somehow entered into a new reality until the subtle terror of being in unknown circumstances dawns upon them. On the other hand, some of them may come deliberately.

In the year 1293, an unknown man who spoke no known language appeared out of the blue during the wedding of King Alexander of Scotland. His apparition was considered an omen, but his subsequent fate did not go down in history. A more ominous character was supposedly seen by thousands in the year 1125. Again, he spoke an unknown language and reportedly shot balls of flame powerful enough to set trees ablaze. More recently, author Richard Popkin's *The Second Oswald* mentioned the appearance of an identical double for President Kennedy's assassin, who showed up at a public shooting range and fired off a strange weapon that produced balls of flame – a curious similarity.

In the late 1960s, two enigmatic individuals checked into a Miami hotel for an extended stay and befriended the chambermaid in the process. When the woman asked her where they were from, the men replied that they hailed from "the north of the continent," stressing that they did not mean the lands north of the United States. The chambermaid and her husband detailed their experiences to paranormal researcher Salvador Freixedo. One of the men was tall and blond, with a command of many languages and telepathic abilities. His sidekick was short in stature, Asian-looking, and wore an orange-colored uniform. He gave the impression of being a retainer or bodyguard to the other man.

According to the chambermaid, the blond produced what appeared to be a ball and stuck it to the wall in defiance of gravity. He then asked the woman to address it, which she did, noticing swirling waves of light within the device, which would follow her in the air every time she made a move. The chambermaid and her husband witnessed the activities of the tall blond and his companion on the beach during stormy weather, pointing what appeared to be cameras and other devices at the rough seas. While cleaning their rooms (the pair refused to leave their rooms while she cleaned), the chambermaid noticed a suitcase filled with "billiard balls" pulsating with light, as if filled with electricity. The two strangers disappeared as suddenly as they had come.

What did the strangers mean by "the north of the continent"? Due to the curvature of the Earth, is it reasonable to assume that they might have meant the lands to the north of the Americas – the polar ice pack and Asia? Freixedo supports the view that the strange men referred to other-dimensional planes of existence accessible through certain materialization-dematerialization points.

The decidedly non-tourist activities of this bizarre twosome inevitably leads us to the notorious Men in Black, whose activities have become a staple of ufology. While MIB activity is usually attached to UFO sightings and occupant encounters, some instances of MIB apparitions are totally unrelated to the phenomenon.

These cases involve such MIB statements that indicate their provenance as being "The Nation of the Third Eye," cited in John Keel's *Our Haunted Planet* (1971; 1999). Although Keel attaches an occult meaning to the statement, could we suspect that they make reference to a physical country located "elsewhere"?

A Pittsburgh MIB case examined by researcher Mike Lonzo in 1995 involved an elderly woman who witnessed the fall of "a strange black stone" into her back yard, an event that was almost immediately followed by a visit from a pair of tuxedo-clad MIBs who demanded the return of the black stone, claiming that its loss would "bring about the destruction of their universe."

Even earlier, in November 1973, a young woman working for an employment agency in San Juan, Puerto Rico, was visited by a man clad in an immaculate black suit with a shirt that seemed to be woven "of a texture unknown on Earth," in her words. The man had extremely long, tapering fingers and a smooth complexion. The woman found herself mesmerized by his conversation, which ranged from the ecology to war, along with statements such as "there were other worlds than this one."

Once we suppress the hair-trigger urge to associate the MIB to UFOs, we see that their motives in these cases were other than silencing saucer witnesses. Could the MIB be able to come and go at will between our world and theirs? That would certainly explain cases in which the sudden disappearance of MIB or their shiny black vehicles have been reported.

Paranormal researcher Brad Steiger, who has written a fair share of books on the subject of out-of-place objects and people, cites an interesting epistolary exchange with a man supposedly able to enter these other levels of existence at will in *Strange Disappearances* (1972). Missourian Al Kiessig wrote the author at length about his experiences with dimensional doorways or "points of access" into other realities.

Kiessig informs Steiger that one of our "neighboring universes" is a soundless environment lacking wind or sun, although its sky is bright enough to suggest the existence of one, and that he himself entered into it while taking his dog for a walk in Arkansas in December 1965. This silent world appeared to mimic our own countryside, down to the wood-frame houses Kiessig encountered along his walk, but the silence and lack of animals or humans was distressing. There appeared to be a considerable time difference between dimensions as well.

Steiger's correspondent went on to mention an unnamed region of the Ozarks in which he could clearly see into the other dimension and watch its inhabitants effortlessly coming into our own. Kiessig stated his belief that this parallel dimension was "the Hell on Earth where Jesus went to preach for three days before he ascended to heaven." According to Kiessig, other dimensional doorways "open into a land of no life. Some take you back into the past, and some take you into the future on this world."

Was the correspondent a teller of tall tales having a laugh at Steiger's expense? A lunatic? Or was he truly gifted with the ability to enter and return from these *dwipas*?

The lesser triangle of forces

Metaphysical anthropology – a contradiction in terms, another bit of New Age claptrap designed to make skeptics' eyeballs ache.

Not so, according to the many thousands of South Americans who have expressed a belief in the theories set forth many decades ago by the late Prof. Guillermo Terrera, a man who appears to have lived his life in a middle realm between harsh reality and the possibility that other realms of existence coexist within our own.

"The enigma has been before us for a very long time," writes Terrera in his book *El Valle de Los Espíritus*, "and both hermetic science and metaphysics make reference to cosmic lights or forces manipulated by the higher intelligences which have plowed Planet Earth's skies for millennia, or else find shelter in subterranean locations, or else moving about in dimensions completely unknown to the ancestral mind of the human species."

Terra posited the existence of a number of interdimensional and/or subterranean realms having a physical "double" in our prime reality. Thus, Thule in the North would have a double in the Antarctic realm, although not necessarily in this dimension. The oft-mentioned Shamballah of Asian tradition would also have a physical counterpart in our world! Most important of all these cities is Erks, located within "the Lesser Triangle of Forces"; a triangle formed by the hills of Calaguala, the village of Serrezuela, and the Cerro Colorado, all of which are found in Argentina's Cordoba province. Basing himself upon the legends of tribes native to the area, the metaphysicist claims that the regents of Erks may allow certain individuals from our reality to find their way there, after achieving a higher intellectual capacity.

The city of Erks, "whose entrances no man has discovered," according to Terrera, features three colossal mirrors constructed from a variety of materials. One of them is made of lapis lazuli, and the others of elements unknown to man. Terrera states that reports of a ghostly white light often reported in the hilltops of the region are produced by Erks and its mirrors.

While Erks thrives in its own unassailable dimension, St. Brendan's Isle seems unstable enough to stumble out of its own and into ours every so often.

Since the 1500s, sailors have reportedly seen an island that appears to fade in and out of our reality in the waters of the Canary Islands. Those who have seen it from afar, and the few lucky ones to have landed on it and managed to leave it, have described it as a mountainous, vegetation-covered island featuring a few rivers. This "eighth" island in the Canarian Archipelago has traditionally been identified as St. Brendan's Isle, after the medieval Irish monk whose adventures on the high seas first brought him to the place. While geographers balk at taking the book about St. Brendan's exploits (the *Navigation Sancti Bendani Abbatis*) as a reliable authority, it is nonetheless interesting that ancient cartographers such as Ptolemy had noted that the Canary Islands had an eighth island – Aprositus – which was "inaccessible." Did the Alexandrian astronomer mean that it was surrounded by deadly reefs, or something more elusive?

In 1570, a Spanish governor received sworn statements from over a hundred Canarian settlers that they had seen St. Brendan's Isle to the north of the island of Hierro and were "even able to see the sun setting behind the isle's peaks." Perhaps even more compelling was the testimony of a skilled Portuguese navigator who reached the island to restock his ship's water stores. There were signs of farm animals and cultivation, and perhaps more ominously, evidence of giant footprints, twice the size of a normal man's. A sudden storm caused the navigator to raise anchor, but after the meteorological phenomenon had subsided, the island could not be found again.

A captain of the Spanish Fleet allegedly reached St. Brendan's Isle and explored it, but again, a sudden storm and the feeling that the island was "moving" caused him to return to his ship.

These may be little more than charming sea stories, but St. Brendan's Isle will not go away. Canarian author Jose Gregorio Gonzalez reports that the island was seen by three fishermen in 1936, seen again in August 1956, and photographed in 1958. Gonzalez admits that the St. Brendan sightings could be an optical illusion – the reflection of the island of La Palma seen under certain optical conditions, but he cautions: "The other theory leads us to subjects related to other dimensions and parallel universes, involving the sudden opening of 'windows' to other worlds of an uncertain nature. For many decades now, the Canary Islands have been identified as one of those special areas in which it is possible to make contact with other dimensions."

In 1983, Rosa and Eva Ledon claimed to have seen St. Brendan's Isle "rising from the sea" one afternoon from their vantage point on Grand Canary. The new island occupied a space between the solid islands of Gomera and Hierro and remained visible for two hours. When the women checked the next morning, it was gone. Researcher Emiliano Bethencourt, who discovered the Güimar Pyramid complex on Grand Canary, interviewed an old man who allegedly saw the interdimensional island in the 1950s, describing it as "a great city with enormous buildings whose lights changed colors."

Unknown dimensions

Scientists are beginning to suggest the possibility that such dimensions, believed to be "curled up" within our own, exist beyond space-time and can be accessed only when energy at the very high or low frequencies is aimed at them. In 1921, Theodor Kaluza presented a paper which posited the existence of a fifth dimension in addition to Einstein's three spatial and one temporal dimensions; in the 1980s, John Schwartz and Michael Green's "superstring" theory proposed a universe of 10 dimensions, six of which were compacted following the Big Bang. According to the researchers, these dimensions are impenetrable and completely unknown to us, but many others, and the witnesses to the events and phenomena described in this article, would beg to differ.

Scott Corrales: Frequent contributor to FATE; *editor of* Inexplicata: The Journal of Hispanic Ufology.

FATE November 2001

THE MAN WHO CAME FROM NOWHERE

Ron Edwards

On a crisp winter morning in 1945, an injured man was delivered to the emergency ward of the US Public Health Service Hospital in Boston. A lonely room became his world until destiny claimed him three decades later.

On February 11, 1945, at 2:20 AM the duty nurse glanced through the glass doors and was surprised to see an ambulance moving up the winding, snow-covered driveway. Minutes later, the oddly dressed driver wheeled a stretcher into the emergency room and helped the nurse place the patient on the examining table.

"You will call this man Charles Jamison," the driver said as he left.

Charles Jamison was in bad shape. The nurse postponed the usual paperwork required for admission and alerted the trauma team. A trio of physicians arrived and were startled by the condition of the comatose patient, who appeared to be in his mid-40s. Bluish-white sores and skin lacerations revealed an acute stage of osteomyelitis, a bone disease. Jamison also had suffered a mild stroke, and his back and legs were covered with infected shrapnel wounds.

His cheek revealed a two-inch scar that had been stitched by an amateur. On his left hand, the index finger had been chopped off below the middle joint.

Elaborate tattoos on both arms presented crossed American and British flags and interlocking hearts. The words "US Navy" were clearly seen under the American flag; "United" was under the English flag, but another word that could have been "Kingdom" was faded.

As the doctors worked on Charles Jamison, they sent the nurse to question the ambulance driver. They could not understand why someone had waited so long before bringing the man in for treatment.

The mystery deepened when the nurse returned to the lobby and discovered that the ambulance was gone. Such unethical protocol was unacceptable, and the bewildered nurse called the police. A few hours later they reported that their queries had uncovered another puzzling fact. No ambulance service – private or public – had been sent to the Public Service Hospital in the last three days.

Now completely baffled, she called her supervisor.

"Are you sure it was a private ambulance?" asked the supervisor.

"Well, I'm not sure," said the nurse, "but it would have been marked with a name if it had been a public ambulance. This one was bright blue, but there was nothing printed on the sides."

"What about the driver?"

"He was strange," she said, after thinking for a moment. "He wore a dark blue overcoat. I think it had brass buttons, not like a policeman's… more like a coat worn by an officer on a ship."

Detectives from the Boston police department tried to learn something about the patient from his clothing. The coat and trousers were foreign and old, but in good condition. All labels were intact but faded beyond recognition. The pockets contained no identification cards, papers, or letters that could shed any light on where Charles Jamison had come from.

The nation's most prominent agencies used every resource to solve the puzzle of Charles Jamison. Fingerprints were sent to each branch of the armed forces, the Merchant Marines, and the FBI. All reported negative results.

Police questioned scores of ambulance drivers, but the duty nurse who had admitted Jamison couldn't identify any of them. Further,

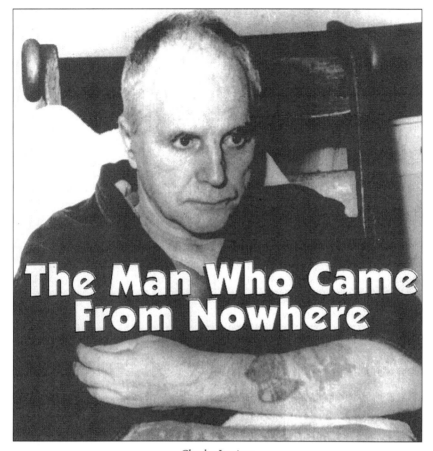

Charles Jamison

no ambulance driver in the Boston area drove the type of vehicle that had delivered Jamison to the hospital.

The silent John Doe

One month after Jamison's perplexing arrival, doctors believed he would survive. Although he was paralyzed from the waist down, his wounds were healing, and he had come out of his coma. His mute state, however, confused the experts. They could not determine if Jamison's silence was caused by his stroke or by psychological trauma.

137

Jamie, as the staff began to call him, was classified a "John Doe," because his name could not be verified.

On July 15, 1945, officials ended the exhaustive investigation without discovering a single clue about their subject's past. It was assumed that Jamison had been a sailor, based on his clothing and tattoos. In reality he seemed to be a man who had never been born.

As weeks turned to months, all attempts to communicate with Jamie were futile. He sat in his wheelchair, staring blankly at the Boston suburb of Brighton beyond his window.

One summer afternoon, a nurse making her rounds looked in on Jamie and saw a scene that rarely changed. Jamison was as much a fixture as the walls and furniture in the small room that was also his prison. Occasionally he smiled, as though some pleasant memory had escaped from a misty region of his mind. As the nurse was leaving, Jamie turned his wheelchair away from the window and said, "I simply do not know." Those five words, spoken with a crisp British accent, were the first he had spoken in more than two years.

The astonished nurse ran down the hall to the duty station. Even while announcing the remarkable change in Charles Jamison's behavior, she wondered if she had actually heard him speak or had just imagined it.

Moments later, Dr. Oliver C. Williams went to Jamison's room. Williams was the hospital's director, but his interest in the quiet patient went beyond medicine; Williams also was a nautical scholar. He decided to become Jamison's personal physician, and he spent many hours with his new patient.

A nautical past

An inspiring plateau had been reached when Jamie broke his silence. Dr. Williams did not know how long the patient would remain responsive, and he quickly summoned his staff for a meeting.

"This may be our last chance to make contact with this amazing man," Williams said. "Somehow, in some way, he has become receptive to questioning."

Dr. Williams' examination began with a series of questions designed to explore Jamison's subconscious in an attempt to reveal his past.

The experiment continued daily. Whenever Jamison answered a question, Dr. Williams would pursue the subject until Jamie could recall no additional details.

During one session Dr. Williams suddenly felt a chill while his patient described historical events. Jamison began to talk about William Gladstone (1809-1898) and Benjamin Disraeli (1804-1881) as if those great English statesmen were still alive.

Next, Dr. Williams sat enthralled as Jamison explained the various campaigns of Napoleon Bonaparte (1769-1821), especially the strategy and troop movements during the Battle of Austerlitz in 1805.

Jamison's fatigue signaled an end to the session and Dr. Williams knew he would have to wait for another day to learn any more.

During the next meeting, Jamison remained silent, so Dr. Williams decided to try another plan to determine his patient's background. The tattoos adorning each arm strongly suggested that Jamison was a sailor.

"What time did you sail, Charles?" He had pushed the right button. Jamison turned around and smiled.

"We cleared the harbor and moved south by southeast. It must have been after midnight, by your time."

A single fact had been clearly established. Charles Jamison had been a sailor. Perhaps more could be learned by limiting the questions to nautical topics.

Back in his office, Dr. Williams called Alton Barker, chief of the British Information Service. He asked Barker to prepare some difficult questions about English ships, customs, and territories.

Questions in hand, Alton Barker took a chair across from Jamison, who ignored his guest and gazed out the window.

Instead of asking questions, Barker began rambling, as if he were an old salt spinning yarns to a small boy. He regaled his solemn listener with tales of stirring naval battles and important events in British history.

Jamison sat transfixed in his wheelchair, oblivious to Barker's narration.

As he talked, Barker pulled some posters from his briefcase and placed them along the bed. He explained that British uniforms were a hobby of his, and he proudly displayed drawings of naval sleeve markings covering 50 years.

Jamison idly glanced at his visitor, then began to concentrate on the colorful illustrations. Moments later, he sat erect and glared at Barker.

"How ridiculous can you be, sir?" asked Jamison. "At least four of those uniform markings are false and historically untrue."

Jamison was absolutely correct. Barker had altered and rearranged some of the insignia to test Jamison's memory.

Barker now had Jamison's attention and handed him a stack of photographs depicting British naval bases and ships. Jamison became bored and lapsed into silence. Barker did not want to lose this moment and quickly changed to buildings and pastoral scenes in England. All of the photos had been arranged to move backward in time from the present.

Jamison remained quiet until he saw a Royal Navy ammunition depot. The back of the photo was stamped "Confidential" by British Intelligence.

Charles Jamison became excited and stabbed a trembling finger at the picture. "That's in London!" he cried. "I've been in that building!"

Barker was confused. He glanced at Dr. Williams and shook his head. The photo had been taken in 1890, and the depot no longer existed.

"What you say is not possible," Dr. Williams said gently. "How old are you, Charles?"

"I am now 49."

Dr. Williams sighed. "That photo was taken more than 60 years ago. Even if you had been the minimum legal age for naval service, 18, you would now be nearly 80 years old."

Jamison had another surprise. His eyes glowed and his hands moved vigorously through the air as he spoke about the naval gunnery school in Gosport...in 1850! He vividly described the weapons, ships, number of men, and the restricted areas inside the school.

Jamison's revelations were confirmed as Barker quickly thumbed through the faded pages of an 1890s naval dossier.

Suddenly Jamison moved his wheelchair to a small table and reached for a 1909 edition of *Jane's Fighting Ships*. He put the heavy book on his lap and started turning the pages, searching for a moment in his past. He paused to admire a large warship.

"Aboard the stately *Bellerophon*, I sailed into the rising moon," he said, tears easing from his eyes.

Jamison's hand rested on a full-page photo of the British battleship, HMS *Bellerophon*, commissioned in 1907. She had participated in the Battle of Jutland during World War I.

"I served on the *Bellerophon* when she was new. I remember..." Jamison paused and rubbed his head. "I remember we set a westward course toward Jutland."

Dr. Williams looked bewildered. "Were you in that battle, Charles?"

"We were in a convoy under secret orders. We had no names on the ships, just numbers." Jamison looked at Dr. Williams, then at Barker. "Even if I knew the sailing codes, I would not tell you."

Incredible! Jamison was reacting as though he were being interrogated by enemy intelligence officers. His attentive guests went along with the charade.

Barker leaned over Jamison. "How many English ships were sunk?"

"If any ships were sunk, I didn't see them."

Jamison had given the standard answer required by naval regulations, but the response disturbed Dr. Williams. Was it possible Jamison did not know that World War I had been over since 1918? Did he really believe the present time to be nearly 30 years ago?

Memories of a bygone battle

Dr. Williams and Alton Barker continued asking questions about Jutland and the *Bellerophon*, but the patient remained silent. Apparently, Jamison, along with other sailors in the Royal Navy, wanted to forget about that critical battle. It was a severe blow to morale, and it signaled the first hint that Britain's powerful fleet was no longer invincible.

The Battle of Jutland was fought off the coast of Denmark on the afternoon and evening of May 31, 1916. Vice Admiral Reinhard Scheer, commanding the German fleet of 99 ships, used new turning-maneuver tactics and searchlights at night to damage the British armada of 151 ships. Admiral Sir John Jellicoe relied on daytime attacks with column formations, a method that had not changed since the British victory at Trafalgar more than a century earlier.

Nearly 112,000 tons of England's finest went to a watery grave, while the superior Royal Navy sank only 62,000 tons. When Britain's heavily damaged vessels limped into port, the weary sailors were booed by shipyard workers. Britannia no longer ruled the waves.

Alton Barker asked Jamison whether his tattoos had a special meaning.

A smile spread across the former sailor's face as he pulled his sleeves back and extended his arms. "These are the markings of a British ensign and an American shield. It symbolizes friendship between the two nations. It is also the symbol worn by the crew of the good ship *Cutty Sark*."

"Was that a battleship, too?" asked Dr. Williams.

Jamison shook his head. "She was a three-masted clipper that sailed the seven seas. She was designed for speed and carried a huge spread of sail."

A few phone calls proved the existence of the vessel, but the truth also made it nearly impossible for Charles Jamison to have been a crew member.

The *Cutty Sark* was a majestic clipper ship from the romantic age of billowing sails and legendary races on the high seas. Launched in 1869 in Dumbarton, Scotland, she cruised with other fast-sailing ships in the English-Chinese tea trade. When the Suez Canal opened, even the fastest clippers could not compete with steamships, which could make the Far East journey in less time. Consequently, in 1872, the *Cutty Sark* became engaged in the Australian wool trade. She was sold to a firm in Lisbon in 1895 and suffered severe damage in a hurricane off the Cape of Good Hope. Another ownership change in Portugal turned the tea clipper into a hauler of scrap iron.

In 1922 Captain William H. Dowman returned her to British ownership where she served as a training ship for 15 years. During World War II she survived England's blitz while permanently docked at the Nautical Training College in Greenhithe.

Queen Elizabeth II proclaimed the *Cutty Sark* a maritime antique in 1957, and the great clipper ship was placed in a dry berth along the Thames at Falmouth Harbor.

A returning POW?

A newspaper article about the mysterious seaman at the Boston hospital caught the attention of a Merchant Marine officer who had formerly served aboard a troop transport.

"Check out the manifest for the USS *Lejeune*," he told Dr. Williams during a phone call. "I seem to remember a man named Jamison."

Detectives trying to find a clue to Charles Jamison's past had tried everything – except a troop ship bringing servicemen back to the United States after the war.

A US Immigration and Naturalization Service investigator found a strange notation in the official documents of the USS *Lejeune*. The ship's manifest said that Charles William Jamison had been picked up at sea, time unknown. He was assigned to the *Lejeune's* manifest out of Southampton, England, on January 24, 1945, and arrived in Boston on February 9, 1945.

At the bottom was written: "Charles William Jamison, July 17, 1895, Boston, Mass., Catholic, four years in a German POW camp in Belgium."

The most puzzling aspect was the manner in which the information about Jamison was recorded. The *Lejeune's* manifest was properly typed and signed by the ship's officers, with one glaring exception: All data about Charles Jamison had been written by hand in ink.

The *Lejeune's* former captain was located and shown the document. He was surprised but unable to offer an explanation. It was against procedure to hand-write names on a prepared roster. He was certain that the handwritten portion about Jamison had not been there when the transport sailed from Southampton.

Efforts were made to find out who had written the notation. Did anyone remember seeing Charles Jamison aboard the USS *Lejeune*? Had anyone seen an ambulance take him from the ship two days after docking in Boston? All roads ended in more dead ends.

The official record said Jamison had been a prisoner of war, picked up at sea. The author of that statement did not suggest how Jamison came to be adrift at sea, or how long he had endured such a fate before he was rescued, or what vessel rescued him, or what caused his serious wounds. The shroud that conceals a mystery is not always woven from cloth. Sometimes the fabric is apathy.

Dr. Williams showed Jamison a picture of the USS *Lejeune*, but he only stared vacantly and said nothing.

The Bureau of Vital Statistics pored over thousands of records going back to 1890. Charles William Jamison's name could not be found among any birth certificates in Massachusetts. Authorities in Washington reported no person by that name in the files of naturalized citizens.

Despite the growing collection of evidence, the search for the truth became even more confusing. Somewhere in the maze of documents there must be answers to explain the enigma of Charles Jamison.

Then another provocative dispatch arrived.

Dr. Williams had requested a history of the *Cutty Sark* from *Lloyds Register of Ships*. Attached to the chronicle from London was a puzzling account from the log of a German submarine.

According to the German High Command, the crew of the U-24 was astonished to see an ancient threemasted clipper ship when they surfaced on the morning of July 10, 1941. Gilded letters on the wooden ship's bow read *Cutty Sark*.

An order was given for the ship to stand by and be boarded, but the vessel turned away with guns blazing from her deck.

Minutes later a torpedo sent the beautiful sailing ship beneath the waves. The submarine's crew saw a few bodies and pulled a sole survivor from the flotsam. That man, named Charles William Jamison, was taken to a German port and then transferred to a German POW camp in Belgium.

Dr. Williams could not believe what he was reading. It was impossible, and yet this news from the German High Command seemed to confirm the remarks about Jamison on the *Lejeune*'s manifest.

No one could explain how Charles Jamison could have been aboard a sailing ship that had not been at sea in more than 20 years. No one could explain how the German report found its way into the Lloyd's document. There was no explanation for the bizarre events described in the log of the U-24. And no one could explain how the *Cutty Sark* could be torpedoed by a German U-boat in the North Sea when she had spent the entire war at a dock in Greenhithe, England.

Eulogy for an enigma

A few months later, while Dr. Williams was talking to his patient, Jamison picked up a note pad and wrote a single word: *Hinemoa*.

"Was that another ship you were on, Charles?"

Jamison nodded. "The *Hinemoa* was a cargo ship that carried nitrates from Chile to British ports. I was aboard when she was sunk by a German submarine." Those were the last words Charles Jamison ever said.

Lloyd's files reveal that the only vessel named *Hinemoa* was a small freighter built by Scott & Company in Greenock, Scotland, in 1876. It was owned by D. W. McKay, and its home port was Wellington, New Zealand.

The *Hinemoa*'s fate differs from the version in Charles Jamison's memory. The SS *Hinemoa* survived World War II and was acquired by the navy as a hulk. In 1945 it was towed to sea and sunk with a demolition charge.

Charles Jamison spent the remainder of his life sitting quietly in his spartan room, staring out the window.

Jamison died on January 19, 1975. About 100 people attended the funeral service at the Seamen's Bethel in New Bedford. Mourners and dignitaries included an honor guard, the mayor, and several coast guard officers.

Everett S. Allen, then assistant editor of the *New Bedford Standard-Times,* gave the eulogy. He eloquently expressed the feelings of those who had come to know the unknown seaman during the last three decades.

"You are here because of one of the most ancient and profound reactions of man," Allen said, "a response to the unspoken need of one man who was alone, and alone in the most unusual sense – he did not even have an identity.

"We have acknowledged that a name is less important than an affirmation of brotherhood. This man is welcome here. Both historically and in terms of contemporary society, he is among friends. He is now at home, regardless of wherever his home may have been."

No one could be sure of Jamison's religion, so the service was ecumenical. No one could be sure of his nationality, so the casket was draped with a Union Jack and an American flag. Everyone knew he had been a man of the sea, and Jamison was buried in the Mariners' Plot of Rural Cemetery.

Years earlier, when Dr. Williams realized that Jamison would never speak again, he told his staff, "I think we will have to give up any hope of solving the riddle of this man. He is beyond the amnesia stage, and his memory is beyond the day he regained consciousness here. I feel he will go to his grave an unknown man."

The prophecy came true.

Ron Edwards: Journalist and writer for radio, television and magazines; author of The World's Most Mysterious Ghost Stories.

FATE March 1997

They Disappeared into the Unknown

Leslie E. Wells

There are numerous cases on record which suggest that men, both singly and in large numbers, have been spirited from the earth.

This seems fantastic. Nevertheless, even famous men, men who had the eyes of the world upon them, have disappeared and years of painstaking search have failed to reveal even a clue concerning their whereabouts.

One of the most famous of these vanished men is John Andruss. John Andruss made the startling claim that he had discovered a secret method of making petrol from water. It seemed impossible, but he was able to convince the authorities that his claim was valid. He convinced them so thoroughly that the British Cabinet appointed a body of experts to make exhaustive tests of the claim. Three experts were chosen: two were British, one being from the Admiralty, and the third was an American attached to the United States Navy.

All three were convinced that John Andruss's claim could only be false. In spite of this he persuaded them that he had indeed discovered a simple method of manufacturing petrol from water. The report concerning the secret, which was sent to America, so impressed the authorities that they placed 250,000 pounds to John Andruss's credit.

All were satisfied that Andruss had provided irrefutable proof of his claim. However, it was decided to apply more stringent tests, under conditions which made trickery impossible. Such tests had already been carried out in Britain. Now they were carried out in America, the first in the presence of Andruss himself. In this test a motorboat had its fuel tank filled with ordinary sea water. The men responsible for this were above suspicion. Then, Andruss poured into the tank a cupful of his secret mixture. No one really expected the boat to move, but, to their astonishment, the craft sailed smoothly over the water.

The experts were impressed but dazed by the remarkable efficiency of the mixture. Nevertheless, they wanted a final test carried out on land. The Indianapolis Speedway was chosen for the experiment. The mixture proved to be just as successful with an automobile as with the speedboat.

John Andruss was not there to see his compound vindicated. He had, to all intents and purposes, vanished into thin air! This was in 1919.

The most intensive search has been made to discover the whereabouts of John Andruss but no trace of him or his body has ever been found. Yet he had no reason for running away. He was already famous and had a fortune to his credit. Even had he wished to disappear, he would have found it hard for he was in the public eye.

The theory is advanced that there were interested persons who wished to destroy him and his secret at the same time. Still it is hard to believe no single clue would be left. At any rate, the mystery of what happened to John Andruss remains. Did he enter another time circle, break through to another plane of existence?

Such an explanation is suggested by other disappearances seemingly even more unlikely.

The case of Owen Parfitt is one of these. Owen Parfitt lived in the little village of Shepton Mallet, Somerset, England. It is a sleepy, isolated place in which a birth is news and a death is an event. Yet something happened there to Owen Parfitt in 1939 that still makes people shiver.

Do people who disappear open a doorway to another dimension?

Parfitt was an ex-sailor who was paralyzed in both legs. He had been unable to walk as much as a step for years. He spent much of his time sitting in a wheelchair in the garden of his home where he was cared for by his sister, a quiet, unimaginative woman, but one who had all her faculties and all her wits.

The two were in the garden one evening when Owen Parfitt complained that he was beginning to feel cold. He asked his sister to bring him a scarf from the house. She entered the house to get the scarf, being absent from the garden not more than a couple of minutes, perhaps less. Returning, she was shocked to the point of collapse to see that the wheelchair was empty. There was no sign of her brother, either in the garden or beyond it. A rug which had been wrapped about his legs remained and so did his pipe. But of Owen Parfitt himself not a trace has been found from that day to this.

Within a short time his sister had informed the police and roused the village, but no one had seen Owen Parfitt, nor had anyone noticed the presence of strangers. Not a soul could give even a scrap of helpful information. The woods nearby were searched thoroughly, trees were investigated, all long grass was cut. Every stretch of water in the area – none was deep – was dragged. No trace of Owen Parfitt was found.

It is impossible to believe that Parfitt disappeared of his own free will. Even had he been pretending, for some reason, that his legs were paralyzed – and this has never been suggested – he had not used them for such a long time that he could not have forced them to run. And he had no reason to disappear. He was not in debt, and everything indicated that he had accepted his inactive life and was quite content.

This leaves only the possibility of foul play. It seems unlikely that he had any enemies in the village for he was unable to mix with the people. His only associates were friends who came for an occasional chat. It might be that he had made an enemy while at sea and that this person had traced him after a considerable lapse of time. But if this is the case, Owen Parfitt must have known his enemy. It was broad daylight and Parfitt must have seen him approach. Why didn't he cry out? His sister had not heard a sound.

Even if Parfitt was knocked unconscious and his body was carried to a waiting car, the mystery remains. For his sister heard no car, either stopping or starting up. Nor did anyone in the village notice a strange automobile as they certainly would have done had one been present.

Was Owen Parfitt suddenly translated to another plane of existence? Is there any significance in Parfitt's last remark that he was feeling cold? Did this herald a change in his bodily makeup which ended in his passing into another world? There is no other explanation with a scrap of evidence to support it.

Equally mysterious is the disappearance of Victor Grayson, British Member of Parliament for Colne Valley. Victor Grayson was a prominent public figure, noted for his abilities as a public speaker. There were those who predicted that he had a brilliant future as an MP. It was said that he would achieve the rank of a Cabinet Minister.

Born in Liverpool, he had had an exciting career which started with his running away from home to become a stowaway. Returning to England, he became an engineer, preacher and journalist and, finally, a Member of Parliament. He was educated at Queen's College, Oxford, attending the lectures that Lord Woolton, the famous Conservative leader, attended.

Well known as an orator, Victor Grayson spent much of his time addressing political meetings in London. He left home in June 1922, to speak at one of these, apparently in the best of health, with no financial or domestic worries, and was never seen nor heard of again.

He did not reach the meeting where he was scheduled to speak. Yet why should he disappear of his own free will when he had such a promising career ahead of him? If he was murdered, how was he killed unnoticed in the crowded London streets? How is it no trace of his body has ever been found? And why was he killed? No one has yet suggested a reason.

Of course he was a politician and would, therefore, have political enemies. But the British dispose of their politicians without bullets, by means of the ballot box. Did Victor Grayson suddenly enter the unknown? The evidence suggests this may well have happened.

Perhaps it is not too surprising that individuals disappear and never are found. But during the Spanish War of Succession, 1701-1714, 4,000 well-trained, fully equipped men marched into the Pyrenes mountains and have never been heard of since.

No solution to their disappearance has ever been found. No satisfactory suggestion has ever been made to account for their vanishing from the face of the earth. They might have fallen prisoners to their enemies, but this seems unlikely for no report of their capture was received.

Did the 4,000 Spaniards freeze to death? This is possible but where are their bodies? Were they overwhelmed by an avalanche? This, too, is possible, but no avalanche was discovered by those who searched for the lost army. Could they have fallen into a hidden pass or crevice? Surely not all 4,000 of them!

The 4,000 men literally marched out of this world.

A similar mass disappearance occurred in 1940. Three thousand Chinese soldiers were sent to fight the Japanese. They just disappeared. The Japanese never claimed them prisoners, never claimed the Chinese deserted en masse. All enquiries have failed to provide a single clue to the missing 3,000 Chinese soldiers.

Six-hundred-and-fifty French troops disappeared in 1858 while marching on Saigon, in French Cochin-China. Disturbances had broken out in Saigon. To restore order the French sent 500 French Legionnaires and 150 first-class Spahis to the city. Not one of these men returned! Not one of these men reached the city!

They were seasoned, experienced troops, not likely victims for an ambush. Even in an ambush not all would have been killed and captured. In any case, word of such a decisive engagement would have come back to the French authorities. The curious thing is, that not a single native of Saigon ever saw a single man of the expedition. In fact, no one ever saw them again after they marched out of their quarters.

Where did they go? Into another world?

The scientific theory of the relativity of time supports such a conclusion. According to this theory, many worlds exist side by side rather than in succession. The mind and spirit are not as much prisoners of a period as we have imagined. And passage from this world to others may well be possible, sudden and unexpected.

FATE July 1956

THE AIR MARSHAL AND THE UNEXPLAINED

Herb Kugel

A group photograph clearly showing the face of a dead man, a terrible airplane flight through a storm into another reality, and a frightening, death-predicting dream were for British Royal Air Force (RAF) officer Sir Robert Victor Goddard glimpses into the world of the mysterious. Goddard (1897-1987), who was known as Victor Goddard, was a senior commander in the Royal Air Force during World War II. He was known for his interest in paranormal phenomena.

The smirking airman

Goddard's first venture into the world of the unexplained involved a photograph. In 1975, the 78-year-old retired air marshal published the story of a photograph that he had kept for many years. It was a group photograph of his squadron. It was taken in early 1919 at the end of

The deceased Freddy Jackson in his squadron photo taken on the day of his funeral

World War I and portrayed some 200 men and women who survived the fighting. It was an official RAF photograph. Nobody could have tampered with either the photograph or its negative at any time. When the photo was developed, it was placed on the squadron bulletin board so that those who wanted copies could sign up for them.

There was one thing wrong, though. There was an extra face in the photograph, a face belonging to the late Airman Freddy Jackson. Jackson was a mechanic, who died by heedlessly walking into a spinning propeller two days before the squadron, which was to be disbanded, posed for the photo. In fact, his funeral took place on the day the squadron gathered for the photo. In the photo, everyone is wearing a hat but Jackson. Everyone is looking grim except Jackson, who is smiling enigmatically. The others had reason to look grim – they had just returned from Jackson's funeral.

Is the face in the photo really that of Jackson's spirit? Goddard and others of the squadron were convinced that it was. Goddard, in his book *Flight Towards Reality*, suggests that Jackson's expression seemed to

154

say: "My goodness me – I nearly failed to make it – They didn't wait, or leave a place for me, the blighters!"

A flight through time

Goddard's second trip into the unexplained involved an airplane flight. This was a much more personally harrowing experience. In 1935, while a Wing Commander, Goddard flew a Hawker Hart biplane to Edinburgh, Scotland, from his home base in Andover, England, for a weekend visit. On the Sunday before flying back, Goddard visited an abandoned airfield in Drem, near Edinburgh, which was closer to his final destination than the airport at which he landed.

The Drem airfield, constructed during the First World War, was a shambles. The tarmac and four hangars were in disrepair, barbed wire divided the field into numerous pastures, and cattle grazed everywhere. It was now a farm, and completely useless as an airfield.

On Monday, Goddard began the flight back to his home base. The weather was dark and ominous, with low clouds and heavy rain.

Air Marshal Victor Goddard

Goddard was flying in an open cockpit over mountainous terrain without radio navigational aids or cloud-flying instruments. Rain beating down on his forehead and onto his flying goggles badly obscured his vision. He thought he could climb above the clouds, but he was wrong. He made it to 8,000 feet, looking for a break in the clouds. There was none.

Suddenly Goddard lost control of his plane. It began to spiral downward. He struggled with the controls. He could speed up or slow down, but he could not stop the spin. He was unsure of his location, but knew he was falling rapidly and might smash into the mountains before coming out of the clouds. The sky became darker and the clouds turned a strange yellowish-brown. The rain came down even more heavily. Goddard's altimeter showed he was only a thousand feet above the ground and dropping rapidly. At 200 feet and still spiraling downward, he began to see a bit of daylight through the murky gloom, but his spiral toward seemingly inevitable death was far from over.

Goddard was now flying at 150 miles per hour. He emerged from the clouds over "rotating water" that he recognized as the Firth of Forth. He was still falling. Suddenly, he saw directly before him a stone sea wall with a path, a road, and railings on top of it. The road seemed to be slowly rotating from left to right. The cloud cover was down to 40 feet. Goddard was now flying below 20 feet and was within an instant of tragedy. A young girl with a baby carriage ran through the pouring rain. She ducked her head just in time to avoid the wingtip. Goddard succeeded in leveling out his plane after that. He barely missed striking the water after clearing the sea wall by a few feet.

He was now flying only several feet above a stony beach. Fog and rain obscured all distant visibility, but Goddard somehow located his position. He identified the road to Edinburgh and soon was able to discern, through the gloom, the black silhouettes of the Drem Airfield hangars ahead of him, the same airfield he had visited the day before. The rain became a deluge, the sky grew even darker, and Goddard's plane was shaken violently by the turbulent weather as it sped toward the Drem hangars – and into a different world.

Suddenly, the sky turned bright with golden sunlight. The rain and the farm had vanished. The hangars and the tarmac appeared to have somehow been rebuilt in a brand-new condition. There were four planes lined at the end of the tarmac. Three were standard Avro 504N trainer

Goddard flew a Hawker Hart on his strange flight

biplanes; the fourth was a monoplane of an unknown type – the RAF had no monoplanes in 1935. All four airplanes were bright yellow. No RAF airplanes were painted yellow in 1935. The airplane mechanics were wearing blue overalls. RAF mechanics never wore anything but brown overalls when working in hangars in 1935.

It took Goddard only an instant to fly over the airfield. He was only a few feet above the ground – just high enough to clear the hangars – but apparently none of the mechanics saw him or even heard his plane. As he sped away from the airfield, he was again engulfed by the storm. He forced his plane upward, flying at 17,000 feet and then, for a time, at 21,000 feet. He managed to return to his home base safely. Goddard felt elated when he landed. He then made the mistake of telling fellow officers about his eerie experience. They looked at him as if he were drunk or crazy. Goddard decided to keep silent about what had happened to him. He did not want a discharge from the RAF on mental grounds.

In 1939, Goddard watched as RAF trainers began to be painted yellow and the mechanics switched to blue coveralls. The RAF introduced a new training monoplane exactly like the one he had seen in his flight over Drem. It was called the Magister. He learned that the airfield at Drem had been refurbished.

Another 27 years went by, but Goddard never forgot what had happened. He played it through over and over in his mind. It was not until 1966 that he wrote of this experience. Over the years he had become convinced that there was no way he could have known that the RAF would change the colors of their trainers and their mechanics' overalls four years before these changes took place. Goddard finally concluded that he must have glimpsed the future – or even traveled into it – for a brief moment in time.

Was this conclusion so unreasonable? Our senses determine our reality. Goddard was under extreme stress and thought he might die. Perhaps the bonds controlling Goddard's senses cracked for an instant, in the face of mortal danger, freeing him to glimpse another reality.

The skipper's dream

Victor Goddard's third encounter with the mysterious, this time involving a frightening dream, took place in the Far East, just after the end of World War II.

It began at a cocktail party given in his honor. It was a party he would never forget. How would you feel if you were at a cocktail party given in your honor and overheard someone talking sadly but in vivid detail about your death in an airplane crash, and you knew you were going to fly the next day? What would you feel if you had learned at the party that your death had been described in a powerful dream, and the dream accurately predicted events that soon started to take place?

The afternoon cocktail party for Air Marshal Sir Victor Goddard took place in Shanghai in January 1946. The war against Japan had ended five months earlier, and Goddard was transferring to a new assignment. The man who was grimly talking about his death was Captain Gerald Gladstone, commander of the Royal Navy cruiser HMS *Black Prince*. Gladstone's tone of sad certainty instantly collapsed into confusion when he saw the Air Marshal standing a few feet from him.

Goddard smiled at the flustered officer. "I'm not quite dead yet," he said. "What made you think I was?"

Gladstone hesitated before replying but when he did, it was with grim conviction. He told Goddard of a vivid and horrifying dream he had experienced the previous night. Goddard, now quite interested, pressed Gladstone for details, which the naval officer nervously supplied. In the

"Now we are for it!"

The flight that was supposed to be fatal

dream, Goddard and three British civilians – two men and a woman – were flying over a rocky shore, off the coast of either China or Japan. It was evening, and they were flying through a ghastly storm. They had just flown over the mountains when their plane crashed.

"I watched it all happen," Gladstone emphatically confirmed. "You were killed." Gladstone further stated that the crashed aircraft was "an ordinary sort of transport passenger plane. Might have been a Dakota."

Later that evening, at a dinner the British Consul General gave in honor of Goddard, the Air Marshal learned to his surprise and shock that his military flight would also be taking civilian passengers, something not usually done. Goddard had understood that it would be impossible that the plane which had been assigned to take him to Tokyo could also ferry civilians, but this now proved to be the case. There were three civilian passengers: The Consul General, a journalist, and a young female stenographer – two men and a woman, all British, exactly as reported in the dream – who would accompany him. Given the dream, it is easy to understand why Goddard was especially reluctant to allow the young woman to travel with him and face what he began to feel was certain death in a plane crash.

159

Their plane was a Dakota transport – also as indicated in the dream. It left Shanghai for Tokyo early the next morning. There was a terrible flight through clouds, exactly as in the dream, some of it over the mountains of Japan, again exactly as in the dream. The Dakota captain was forced to crash-land his plane in the early evening during a snowstorm. He crashed on the rocky, shingle shore on an island off the coast of Japan, again as in the dream, but this time with one vital difference. Everyone survived.

As time went on, as with the flight over Drem Airfield, Goddard could not get the event out of his mind. On January 2, 1947, about a year after the crash, he wrote Gladstone and asked for more particulars regarding the harrowing dream. In his letter he told the naval officer, "For the next 48 hours I was quite convinced that I was going to die and wondered how many unfortunate passengers would share the experience with me."

Gladstone's reply, dated January 30, 1947, stated in part: "I am sorry to say that I am unable to fill in any details of the dream…I clearly remember now what I remembered of my dream at the time: and that was a conviction that YOU WERE DEAD…I have never made a point… of recalling every detail of my dreams the instant I awake." Gladstone thus claimed to have remembered absolutely none of the details Goddard attributed to him.

Both officers were of unimpeachable character and both agreed that this was a precognitive experience. Why is there a vital difference in their two accounts? There is the possibility that Gladstone related the specific details of his dream to Goddard at the cocktail party and then later forgot both the details and that he had told them to the Air Marshal.

In 1950, four years after the party, Goddard, still disturbed by the event, wrote an article about the incident for *The Saturday Evening Post*. The article, printed on May 26, 1951, was the first time the story became public. Goddard did not use Gladstone's real name or that of his cruiser, but he did send a copy of the manuscript to the naval officer for suggestions and comments before it was printed. Gladstone again stressed that he had not remembered any of the specific details of his dream.

Does that matter? What matters are the awful power and certainty of the dream to the dreamer. Gladstone awoke absolutely convinced that Goddard was dead. All day before the cocktail party the naval officer expected to be informed of the air marshal's death. He only went to the party when no such news was received, but he was still positive of Goddard's death and kept vehemently saying so at the party where the Air Marshal overheard him.

Gladstone also maintained that he had never experienced anything like this dream and remained at a complete loss to explain it. If we also cannot explain it, we still might further wonder why Gladstone experienced it in the first place. If it was meant to be a warning, why was it not sent to someone closer to Goddard, or to Goddard himself?

Is there a bottom line here? Did Gladstone glimpse a future? Was there an alternate or probable future in which a Sir Victor Goddard did indeed perish in an air crash? Gladstone reported that in his dream he "watched it all happen." Just where was he while he was watching?

In 1954, Goddard's experience with Gladstone's dream was made into a British motion picture, *The Night My Number Came Up*, starring Michael Redgrave as Air Marshal "Hardie." Although this is an entertaining film, the scriptwriter made significant changes in regard to the actual events that weakened the power and significance of the true story.

Goddard had two other earlier encounters with the unexplained. In August 1911, while he was an eleven-year-old naval cadet, he learned that his mother was fearful that the "Agadir (Morocco) Crisis" would explode into a world war. German naval units were sent to Morocco to block French expansion in that country and many feared that the crisis would erupt into a war between France and Germany with England then being dragged into it. The young Goddard instantly assured his mother that war would not come until August 1914, which indeed was the case, that being the start of World War I. On August 4, 1914, Goddard, now 14, was watching a sunset from the quarterdeck of a British battleship. He states in the preface to his 1975 book, *Flight Towards Reality*, that he was given a "clear presentation by the cloud movements and their colors in the sky" of how long the war, which was to begin that night, would take and how it would end. He had no idea why these particular events happened to him, but he never forgot them.

Father of ufology?

Air Marshal Sir Victor Goddard had a long and successful career. He joined the Royal Navy in 1910 when he was 13 years old, later transferring to the RAF in 1918. He is thus considered one of the founders of the RAF. As Deputy Head of the RAF Delegation to the United States, he was stationed in Washington, DC from 1946 until 1948. He represented the RAF on the combined Chiefs of Staff Advisory Committee and coined the word "ufology" in 1946 when there was an outbreak of UFO sightings. During this period, he was convinced that UFOs were a hoax. He was instrumental in convincing President Harry Truman (through USAF Chief of Staff Carl A. Spaatz) to halt the US Air Force search for UFOs, a search Truman had ordered to help investigate the rumors of prowlers in American air space.

Goddard later regretted this decision and changed his mind about UFOs after his retirement from the RAF in 1951. In *Flight Towards Reality*, he wrote of his belief in the existence of UFOs and speculated that they might come from a psychic or spiritual world parallel to ours.

After his retirement from the RAF, Sir Victor spent 20 years in research in psychology, psychical research, and healing. He died in 1987 at the age of 90.

FATE July 2000

THE RESTAURANT THAT DISAPPEARED

Debra D. Munn

One of the most baffling supernatural phenomena ever to take place in Wyoming occurred in March 1959. Bob Wetzel (pseudonym) was stationed at Lowry Air Force Base in Denver, Colorado. He and friends John and Dee Greeley (pseudonyms) were driving up to visit Bob's wife, Sharon, who was living in Worland.

Just as the three were leaving the Cheyenne city limits, a blinding spring snowstorm hit. Whereas it normally took only a short time to get from Cheyenne to Chugwater, this trip through the blizzard took an hour and a half. Road conditions kept getting worse and worse, and anyone who has ever traveled on Wyoming highways can appreciate the relief the travelers felt when they were finally able to make out the dim, beckoning lights of a restaurant in the distance.

Here is Bob's story:

We were so glad to find a place to come in out of the storm and have dinner. We pulled off to the left side of the road and walked across the street; then we ran up some steps leading into the building. I believe we went through some swinging doors there in the front, and I remember we were the only three having dinner at the time. The help was there – the cook, dishwasher, and others, but we were the only customers.

The restaurant was quite pleasant, with white linen tablecloths, silverware, and tall water glasses at each place setting. Two young women dressed in long white dresses with black and white aprons waited on us, and to the best of my recollection, John and I both had steaks and Dee had chicken. Each of us also had a beer.

When we finished our meal, we were very surprised to see the tab on our bill. It came to only nine dollars for the three of us! I was so pleased that I left five one-dollar bills as a tip, and you should have seen how surprised the waitresses were! They thanked me, walked us to the door, and told us to be careful, since it was still snowing so hard you could barely see.

Once we got to the other side of Chugwater, however, and close to Douglas, the storm suddenly lifted, and we made it up to Worland without any trouble.

When we got there, we told my wife, Sharon, and her parents about the nice restaurant we'd found, and so we decided to stop there again on our way back to Denver.

When Sharon made the return trip with us, the weather was clear, and we had no trouble getting to Chugwater.

This was before the highways were fixed, and you had to drive right through the middle of the town. I remembered that as we had come down the hill, from Denver heading north, the restaurant had been the third or fourth business on the left-hand side of the street.

But this time it just wasn't there! There wasn't even any building on the site. We were looking at a vacant lot!

Unable to believe our eyes, John and I walked to a nearby hamburger stand, where I spoke to an elderly gentleman. I think his name was Charlie, and I told him we had come through Chugwater and eaten at a restaurant that was no longer there.

"Pardon me?" he asked. "Are you sure this was where you were?"

I said, "I'm positive. That's right where I parked."

"When was this?" Charlie asked, with a funny look on his face.

"Eight to 10 days ago," I told him. And then he dropped the bombshell.

"Son, the place that you describe burned down years and years ago, and this has been a vacant lot since then."

"There's no way!" I said. "We were just in there!" I began to describe both of the waitresses who had served us.

"Son," the man said again, "that place burned down, and the two people you describe perished in the fire. But that was years and years ago."

I looked at John, who had turned a little pale, and he said, "The best thing we can do is get the hell to Denver!"

Back in the car, Sharon made light of the situation, believing that the other three were playing a joke on her. Only when Dee became quite anguished and insisted that they were all telling the truth, did Sharon believe them.

Thirty years on

The stories of the witnesses have never changed. Bob is the first to admit that if he had been alone at the time of the experience, he never would have told anyone about it and would have had serious doubts about his sanity. In fact, on the way back to Denver, the participants in this strange adventure racked their brains for a logical explanation.

"We thought maybe we had never been in Chugwater at all, that maybe we had been in another town," said Bob. "But, hell, there is no other town around there. Because on that road you went from Cheyenne to Chugwater to Wheatland to Douglas to Casper to Worland; we knew that road very well because we travelled it often. Anyway, everything else in the town seemed the same, except that the restaurant was gone.

Looking back on the experience, Bob could recall nothing unusual about the restaurant itself, except for the low cost of the meal. The food and drink seemed real in every way and were much more filling than a mere "ghost" of a dinner would have been. But Bob did remember thinking at the time that the complexions of both waitresses were very white, and later he realized that their long dresses and aprons might have belonged to an earlier time.

Time travel?

How can the experience that had happened to Bob and the Greeleys be explained? Bob insists he doesn't believe in ghosts, but he has no other explanation for what occurred.

Could the snowstorm have confused the three travelers so that they didn't know where they were? That seems unlikely, since they were well acquainted with the route, and since there were no other towns along that particular stretch of road from Cheyenne to Douglas. Could atmospheric or other unknown conditions of that blustery day in March 1959 somehow have triggered a flashback into the past?

Alternate realities

As bizarre as that theory sounds, it may be the most likely explanation, especially when one considers that other, similar stories have been reported. The most famous involved two female Oxford dons who, while visiting Versailles on August 10, 1901, were apparently transported for a short while to the Versailles of an earlier time.

Another such trip into the past was reported in an episode of Arthur C. Clarke's *World of Strange Powers*. In this case, two British couples stayed overnight and had dinner at a French inn that they were unable to locate later. The story is very similar to Bob's, in that some of the inn's other customers were wearing old-fashioned clothes, and the bills for both hotel and restaurant were astonishingly inexpensive.

I corresponded with J. Finley Hurley, the author of a book on inanimate apparitions and "time slips" such as Bob and his friends may have experienced. When I presented the facts of the Chugwater story to him, this was his response:

It would seem that Bob and his companions either blundered into the past or into an alternate present where the restaurant continued to operate, and fashions didn't change – or they were served by apparitions. Concerning the latter explanation, however, there is nothing in the literature of apparitions (including hauntings and such) that could begin to account for the experience. So, I must assume the trio wandered into the past.

The "very white" complexions of the waitresses (a sour note, that) could simply reflect a time not so long ago when women avoided suntans. In any event, apparitions of the dead aren't the deadly white so popular in folklore. Also, assuming ghosts don't charge for their services, the prices would have been appropriate over a considerable span of time, perhaps into the fifties. I think it's possible that they did have the experience reported.

Fact or fiction?

My next step was to try to check out the facts of Bob's story against the early history of Chugwater. Official records before the town's incorporation in 1919 are practically nonexistent, but old-timer Russell L. Staats checked his diary and discovered that on March 25, 1959, Chugwater did, indeed, get nine inches of snow. He also believed that a restaurant had existed at one time in the area Bob described.

Chugwater residents Tim and Peggy Dreas did some further scouting around for me and found another old-timer who said that almost every business, including a restaurant in the locale described by Bob, had burned to the ground in the first part of the century. No one remembered anyone dying in the blaze, however, but someone did remember a man who roamed around town much like the "Charlie" in Bob's account.

Peggy Dreas told me more about this man. "His name wasn't Charlie, but something similar, such as Ollie, perhaps – so it would have been easy to remember it over the years as Charlie. This fellow apparently had no family and spent most of his time downtown walking the street, so it's very possible that Bob could have spoken to him."

There is another interesting footnote to Bob Wetzel's story. Loren Coleman, in his book *Mysterious America* (1983), lists names of people and places that for unknown reasons are involved more often than others in supernatural occurrences. Bob's surname is included in that list. When I informed him of this fact, he laughed and vowed, "Then I'm going to change it to Smith!"

Debra D. Munn: Author of books and articles about ghosts and hauntings in Wyoming and Montana.

FATE August 1992

National, Indiana

Dominic P. Sondy

"Please pass the ketchup, brother," asked the middle-aged man on the stool next to mine. The diner where we were having breakfast was the early morning meeting place. His casual conversation was natural and easy – as if he had known me for years. It may have been typical of this small town where most people knew each other. The first time this happened to me I did not think it too unusual; a total stranger calling me "brother."

Others came and went in and out of the diner, out into the cool, misty rain falling on downtown National, Indiana. Almost everyone greeted each other with comments about the rain, the local high school football score and other small talk. Most of the people used the term "brother," just as the man with the grey mustache and long sideburns did when he thanked me for the ketchup.

The Mercantile Hotel was across the street. Like so many midwestern small towns, the frame building with a wide veranda was a relic of a bygone era. Mostly, it served "drummers" such as myself, who came from northern cities like Chicago, where I worked for a publishing firm.

During the Reconstruction period of the South, businesses sent salesmen to sell the people products. My particular product was lodge organizational advertising, which would appear in various magazines.

Staying at the hotel did not figure into my plans so early in the day. I had two stops to make, and each would take me about an hour. I could be well on my way north early in the afternoon, so I was not planning on staying overnight; at least, not this early in the day.

After my toast and coffee, I walked a half block to my car. Across the street was the Merchants Bank of National. I made a mental note of its location since I might have to cash an expense check before three o'clock when most banks closed for the day.

Since all the towns I covered had a population of 5,000 or less, there wasn't much chance of having trouble finding the only bank in town.

I liked National

A few weeks later, I visited a friend of mine who lived near Lansing, Michigan. As we sat in his living room I just had to tell him all about National, Indiana. "If I ever get to retire, this is the place I would like to settle in."

"Why a small midwestern town?" was the first question my friend Howie asked.

I couldn't wait to tell him about the way the people there made me feel welcome, as if they knew me all my life – even a Yankee salesman from up North. They made me feel welcome more than I ever did in most of the towns I stopped in.

"Wait until I tell you what happened in the barber shop," I said. I related how I had sat there reading a magazine waiting to get a trim. The man sitting next to me said, "Brother, I don't ever remember seeing you here for a haircut before."

I explained that I was a salesman and that I was planning to see the secretary of a certain lodge in about an hour. The barber joined in the conversation and assured me I would have no trouble finding her office as it was only a few blocks away. It became obvious to me that almost everybody knew everyone else in this town.

This was strange. People were helping me find my first contact of the day. Most people resented salesmen who came into their town and tried to sell them something and then take the money out of town.

170

Where is National?

After relating all of this to Howie, he said, "Now, where is this town of National?" He went over to his desk and pulled out an atlas and resettled in his easy chair. He adjusted his reading light, so he could see the small print.

I pulled out my ledger which carried a day-to-day record of all the stops I made, whom I contacted, sales made or not made. I pointed out on the map that the town was north of Indianapolis and south of South Bend. I drove into National as I proceeded on Highway 31 north.

"Heck," Howie said, "this town is so small it's not even on the map."

He was right. It was not on any map you got free at most gas stations in 1960. It certainly was not on the map that I had marked out my route. Since I covered most of the northern half of Indiana that fall, I didn't think too much about it at the time. I didn't bother Howie with all the details of the rest of my stay in town. I went back to do the rest of my scheduled towns after National the following week.

Sales in National

After noon on the day of mystery I kept my first appointment. The lady was very polite but did not buy my advertising program. As I packed up my briefcase she asked me who I was going to see next. She said I could use her telephone to call ahead and confirm my appointment.

I started out the door when she said, "Stop in next year when I am chairman of the lodge, brother."

A short drive took me to the outskirts of town and to a Georgian house. I left my car across the street and started walking to number 66. A girl of about eight or 10 years of age was singing rhymes and playing hopscotch all by herself. This was on the sidewalk next door to number 66.

"Dance with me, brother," she said. She held out her arms as if she wanted me to swing her around by the hands. I thought it was a little strange that this girl was playing a game with the spaces marked out with chalk just like little girls did when I was her age.

The doorbell was the kind you twisted and sounded like a bicycle bell. Not even electric! Mrs. Jessup ushered me into her Victorian living room. After my call she had the coffee all poured out since she knew it would only take me a few minutes to get there from Main Street. We quickly concluded our business and I snapped the locks on my briefcase.

An 18-year-old beauty

A stunning young girl came down the staircase. She was wearing a blue cloth coat and a white knit hat. She was also carrying a white handbag. She appeared to be about 18 years of age. The young freshness of her blonde hair and fair skin was highlighted by the most perfect white teeth I had ever seen. The mother introduced her to me. The girl told her mother that she was on her way downtown to do some shopping. Since it had stopped raining, she had decided to walk.

"Mr. Sondy is going that way," the mother said. "Maybe he wouldn't mind giving you a ride."

As we rode the short distance back to Main Street, I was tempted to keep sneaking peeks at those perfect, white teeth. All too soon the ride was over. I dropped her off in front of the shop she pointed out.

The question that came to my mind was: how could this mother trust a total stranger, whom she had never seen before, with her daughter? Mrs. Jessup's words kept coming back to me after we walked out the door. "Don't forget to come back and see me when you come through here next year, brother."

I stay in National

My curiosity about the people convinced me to stay overnight at the Mercantile. The room was on the second floor and faced the street. One tall, narrow window let in the late afternoon sunlight.

The wallpaper was strangely familiar. Then I remembered – it was the same pattern in the living room of a house my father built in Detroit in 1927.

I walked around the downtown section after dinner in the hotel dining room. As much as I was aware of the old-fashioned air about this town, the cars were still 1960 and before. They did have electricity and most modern conveniences. Many things were consistent with the times. Yet there were things strangely different; sort of outdated or out of the past, such as the 1930-style coat the girl wore, or the long sideburns and mutton chops on the barber.

Most disturbing was the warm, trusting, friendly feeling that came from all the people I met. It was a sincere kind of brotherly love that was not put on for selfish reasons.

There goes that word again, "brother."

172

Did it happen?

I am still not sure all these incidents happened as I remembered them; at least the way I think I remembered them. I have checked with a friend who has lived in Nappanee, Indiana, most of her lifetime. She has never heard of this town or any other with a name that even sounds like National.

I have read and heard of people who allegedly have experiences about places or people who appear as if out of nowhere and disappear just as mysteriously. I have checked many old maps, atlases and zip code directories ever since. I have pondered this experience and thought about writing about it. I have never found National on any Indiana map or listed in any kind of directory. I get no answers, just more questions.

Did the whole town and its people exist for the one fall day I made my visit? If so, why?

FATE February 1991

KLEE... Still Calling

Curtis Fuller

The mystery about a wandering TV signal could be one of the strangest enigmas of modern times. Electronic experts have tried to solve it without any luck. It even has been suggested that the proper explanation is a mix-up in time. The most recent information on reception of KLEE-TV signals was made available to FATE by Frank Edwards, author of the book *Strangest of All.*

There used to be a television station in Houston, Texas called KLEE. In July 1950, KLEE-TV became KPRC-TV. Since then, so far as FATE has been able to learn, there have been no broadcasts, anywhere in the world, of the signals KLEE-TV.

Yet, such signals have been received, not once but repeatedly. And the reception has been reported not from the vicinity of Houston but from areas as far apart as London, England, and Milwaukee, Wisconsin!

In the fall of 1953 and winter of 1954 Paul Huhndorff, chief engineer of KPRC-TV, received letters from England reporting numerous receptions of the KLEE call letters.

Londoner Charles Batley and Atlantic Electronics, Ltd., of Lancaster, stated that they had picked up the call letters KLEE-TV "many times" between September 14, 1953 and January 8, 1954. They even sent photographs of their TV screens to prove it.

There are two great mysteries here. The first is that television signals ordinarily are not received beyond line-of-sight distances. Unlike ordinary broadcast radio waves, they do not rebound from the ionosphere but usually penetrate it and continue on into space. This is not always true, however, and sometimes electronic conditions are such that TV signals can be reflected from the electronic layers encasing the earth and are received at a great distance.

It is not beyond the realm of possibility, therefore, that signals from a TV station in Texas could be reflected a long distance – perhaps even as far as England.

But that such signals should be reflected repeatedly while other US signals are not reflected seems all but impossible.

An even bigger mystery with the KLEE signals, of course, is that so far as anyone knows the last "official" KLEE-TV signal was broadcast in July 1950 – more than three years before the new "unauthorized" signals began to be reported.

It has been suggested that the signals may be a hoax, but who can afford such a hoax? TV equipment capable of broadcasting such signals, even from point to point within England, would cost tens of thousands, probably hundreds of thousands of dollars. In addition, it is strictly illegal to make such a broadcast, and who would want to risk costly equipment on a pointless venture?

The chief engineer of the British Broadcasting Corporation told newsmen, quoted as follows by Frank Edwards in his book *Strangest of All*:

> *We are confronted in this instance with a set of circumstances which are at variance with accepted knowledge of television transmission. It is unthinkable that these signals could have been circling the earth for the period of time since that station last broadcast them. It is physically impossible that they could have been reflected to us by chance from a celestial body at such a vast distance. That leaves us with but one possibility, however bizarre, that these signals*

176

were transmitted to us purposefully and intelligently, from a source and for a purpose presently unknown.

Even this might have been forgotten but on November 23, 1955, H.C. Taylor, one of the electronics specialists who had reported the original reception, turned on his TV for long range reception and there were the mysterious letters again: KLEE-TV! And Mr. Taylor, lest we forget, lives in Morecambe, Lancashire, England.

It now seemed unlikely that claims as sensational as this could go unchallenged indefinitely. Sure enough, in February 1960, the "perfect explanation" was offered.

Charlotte Phelan, writing in the *Sunday Houston Post* of February 14, 1960, stated that "an aged inventor in England" had faked the signal and actually had transmitted a copy of a station identification card.

Details, including the name of the "aged inventor," are curiously lacking, but even so, FATE was inclined to accept this explanation, at least provisionally, for want of something better, despite obvious loopholes in the report.

The biggest loophole is that the photographs sent to Engineer Paul Huhndorff at KPRC-TV were identified by him as showing the standard call letter slide actually used by KLEE-TV. How did this anonymous, aged inventor happen to get hold of that slide?

So matters might have rested, if KLEE had not been seen again! In February 1962, exact date not available, Mrs. Rosella Rose of Milwaukee, Wisconsin, tuned in her set and got the station. It was not until June 16 of that year, however, having just finished reading about the mystery in Frank Edwards' book, *Strangest of All*, that Mrs. Rose even realized it was a mystery. Here is what she wrote to Mr. Edwards:

> *I have just finished your* book Strangest of All *and reading it brought to mind something I would like to report.*
>
> *This year, along the last of February, I was trying to get a program on TV for a short rest before starting home from a long day's work. The time was around 7 or 7:30 PM. On turning on the dial I got station KLEE.*
>
> *Of course, I had never heard of the station or didn't know where it was. The KLEE flickered off and on several times before any sound or picture came through.*

> *The picture came first, showing a woman running toward what looked like a balcony. She was followed by a man who caught up with her. They seemed to be talking but at first I couldn't make out what was said or understand it. Then the words came through.*
>
> *The girl speaking said, "Let me go. I'm going to tell the world what you plan on doing!" She was speaking to the man she had been running from who was then holding her by the arms.*
>
> *The picture changed slightly, showing the back head and shoulders of a second man. There was something said then that I couldn't understand, apparently a question by the second man and answers by the girl.*
>
> *Then the second man said, "My God, man, you can't do that. It will be a catastrophe!"*
>
> *The picture faded out then and the KLEE flashed on again, and here's the really strange part: superimposed over the KLEE, which was still on, the word "HELP" flashed on, off, and on again. The screen then went black.*
>
> *I waited to see if it would come on again. It didn't, and it was over a channel we never get a station on here.*
>
> *I was alone at the time, and in closing up for the night I didn't think any more about it until I got home. Then I checked the TV news section in the papers but there was no KLEE listed. So, I thought maybe it was a station farther away and one not listed in our papers here in Milwaukee.*
>
> *Then, on reading your book last night, the chapter "Signals From Space" really knocked me for a loop.*
>
> *What do you make of this?*

There already has been much speculation about this mystery, but if the facts are correct more speculation is certainly warranted.

Men as far apart as flying saucer fans on the one hand, and F. D. Drake on the other, were concerned. Dr. Drake was associate astronomer at the National Radio Astronomy Observatory at Green Bank, West Virginia. Green Bank has been trying to make radio contact with life in other planetary systems, and one of the possibilities was that the KLEE signals had been rebroadcast by other intelligences in space.

This, from a less scientific viewpoint, was also the attitude of the UFO fans, but they suggested that the signals were being rebroadcast by flying saucers orbiting the earth.

Another suggestion, made by Chief Engineer Huhndorff, was that the TV waves may have penetrated the ionosphere into space and been reflected back when they hit a celestial object several light years away. The BBC chief engineer. as stated, believes this to be physically impossible. Furthermore, there are too many reports of this wayward signal being received and it seems most unlikely that an already unlikely one-time accident would be repeated.

Another proposal, likewise rejected by the BBC chief engineer, is that the signals were just wandering around in space all this time until somehow, they found their way back to a few TV sets on Earth.

The same basic objections apply here – the strength of the signals, the repetitious receptions which are too frequent to be coincidental, and the absence of any theory that could account for such wanderings.

An equally far-out theory offered in FATE way back in 1954 is that *time* itself, so little understood, might have folded back and through some trick the signals were received a fraction of a second after they were broadcast on one plane, while three to four years elapsed on another.

We are living in a universe of mystery, and the KLEE enigma reinforces that realization even though it appears to deepen the mystery rather than help solve it.

Curtis Fuller (1912-1991): Co-founder of FATE with Raymond Palmer, publisher and author.

FATE: April 1964

TELEPORtation

TELEPORTATION: SCIENCE FICTION – OR REALITY?

Jeffrey Roberts

"Energize!" We all remember that familiar command given by Starfleet crewmen in the famous television series, *Star Trek*. In an instant individuals or cargo would dematerialize into their component atoms and be beamed onto a strange planet, far below the orbiting USS *Enterprise*. There, the constituent atoms would be magically reintegrated into their original whole form.

In 1966, when the show first aired, such a means of transport filled viewers with awe and wonder. And yet, science fiction writers have used the theme of teleportation (matter transmitter, disintegrater-integrater; call it what you will) for far longer than most people realize. In 1877 author Edward Page Mitchell toyed with the idea in his book *The Man Without a Body*. As early as 1927, Sir Arthur Conan Doyle, creator of the master detective Sherlock Holmes, explored the concept in his story "The Disintegration Machine." Modern day authors have utilized the idea of teleportation in a variety of imaginative ways, such as Isaac Asimov's "It's Such a Beautiful Day," Stephen King's "The Jaunt," "Ringworld" by Larry Niven, "Jumper" by Stephen Gould (which was made into a movie), and numerous others.

Teleportation in the movies

From movies such as *Stargate, Doom,* and *The Terminator,* the theme of teleportation has been an endless source of ideas for writers. From television shows, movies, video games, and books, people never seem to tire of wondering what it would be like to teleport oneself to any point on the globe in the blink of an eye – lunch at an outdoor café in Paris, back to Los Angeles to take your laundry out of the washing machine and fold it – then back to your sunny table in Paris for dessert.

But the concept of actual teleportation has only been fantasy – the realm of science fiction. Jump ahead 40 years or so beyond the *Star Trek* TV show and the line between fantasy and reality may no longer be so clear cut.

What exactly is "teleportation" or "matter transmitter"? We can transmit sound over vast distances instantaneously using carrier waves such as radio broadcasts. That's one-dimensional. And we can transmit electronic images, too, as in television. That's two-dimensional. But, the transmission of a solid object, animate or inanimate, wirelessly, over global distances? That's three-dimensional. Now we're getting into infinitely more complex technology – the transmission not of sounds or images, but of solid matter itself. Would you volunteer to be the first living subject to be teleported 10,000 miles in the blink of an eye? One only has to remember the movie *The Fly* in order to conjure up images that are the stuff nightmares are made of. This did not stop the United States Air Force from undertaking a seven-million-dollar 2004 project entitled "Teleportation Physics Study." At least a dozen companies, plus scientists and universities from the United States, Austria, Denmark and China, are actively pursuing teleportation experiments.

What stage of teleportation are we capable of now? We're a long way from the transporter of Captain Kirk and Jean Luc Picard.

Scientists are experimenting with "quantum teleportation" – more like a "repliporter" of information, rather than solid matter. But it is

Teleportation of the future

a beginning. What researchers are using now to achieve the instantaneous transmission of information, without having to traverse the intervening space, is a strange property called "quantum entanglement." It describes the weird behavior where two particles can have the same properties, and be connected, even though they may be millions of light years apart. Think of two identical tuning forks at opposite ends of a large empty room. When one is struck, the other starts sympathetically vibrating, as well. That is what quantum entanglement is, though on a scale trillions of times greater: a change in one particle is instantly mirrored in the other. New Agers will instantly see the parallel to the philosophy of everything

185

in the universe being interconnected. Albert Einstein called it "spooky action at a distance."

It's not so much teleporting an atom or photon to a distant location, but rather the "reincarnation" of an exact copy of it, at that distant receiver point. This process would also destroy the original, balancing things out. (Bioethicists are having fits, contemplating the unpleasant implications for 22nd-century teleportation of people, if it becomes feasible.) Think of it as a cosmic fax machine. What comes out is not the original, but an exact copy. In 2010, Chinese scientists teleported an ion a distance of 10 miles, a record. Considering that the record a year earlier was only a few yards, the progress is encouraging.

Quantum computation

Ironically, quantum entanglement theory may soon point the way toward the development of, if not teleportation itself, quantum computers, using information-carrying light (quanta) instead of wires to crunch data. Eventually, their inconceivably fast processing power might someday provide the missing component we'll need to scan a human being in a reasonable amount of time, as part of the teleportation process, if we ever wish to teleport people. A quantum computer could quickly perform calculations that would take today's super computers 13 billion years to accomplish.

A daunting task

Might we someday teleport humans across the planet, as well as through space, as easily as we drive to work today? Teleporting a human being, says physicist Eric W. Davis, would require scanning every atom in an individual's body – more than a trillion trillion – using a computer with 1.028 kilobytes of computer storage capacity. You would need one hundred quintillion of today's super computers to scan one human being, and it would take 2,400 times the age of the universe to do it. And to dematerialize one human would require the energy equivalent of 330 one-megaton thermonuclear bombs, adds Davis.

I am reminded of Professor Simon Newcomb, an astronomer who proved that powered flight was impossible. A few months after publishing his paper, a couple of bicycle mechanics – the Wright brothers from Dayton – took off in an airplane. The good professor's problem? His math was perfect. His assumption was flawed. Start out with a false assumption and you'll end up with a false conclusion.

On that blustery day of December 17, 1903, the Wright brothers flew a distance shorter than the wingspan of a modern 747. Yet 66 years later, less than the span of a human lifetime, men walked on the moon. As scientist/author Arthur C. Clarke said, "When a distinguished but elderly scientist states that something is possible, he is almost certainly right. When he states that something is impossible, he is probably wrong." He also said, "Any sufficiently advanced technology is indistinguishable from magic." (It is probably not lost on UFO devotees that certain close encounters of the third kind, as well as abductee cases, report aliens' use of teleportation technology, and it seems to function just fine.)

But who in 1911 could have possibly predicted the scientific advancements we take for granted today? Who can possibly predict the technological wonders coming 100 years from now? Or even 50 years? It is enough just to wonder at the possibilities.

As for myself, I'm going to step into my Acme Mark IX Teleporter now. It's lunchtime, and I know a quaint little outdoor café on Alpha Centauri…

Jeffrey Roberts: Writer and novelist with a master's degree in history from Northern Arizona University.

FATE September-October 2011

I Teleported Home

John Otto

March 28, 1956 was a cold, snowy night in Niagara Falls, New York. I was there on a business trip that had kept me away from Chicago and home for several weeks. It may have been the weather, or it may have been something that had happened in my business; for whatever reason, I had a great yearning to be home. As I stumbled along in the snow toward my rooming house, it occurred to me that a phone call to Chicago might be just what I needed to dispel my awful loneliness.

At the end of the telephone conversation with my wife I told her my work would keep me in the east for at least another two weeks.

I spent the rest of the evening reading, then went off to bed. But I couldn't go to sleep. The yearning to be home had been increased rather than lessened by the telephone call. I never had experienced such homesickness!

I lit my cigarette lighter and saw my watch said 10 PM. I lay thinking fondly of home, of my wife, of my daughter and son, even of our parakeet that customarily joined me when I ate my meals. When my loneliness persisted, I began to visualize mentally a trip back to Chicago and home. I did as the mystics suggest, "go through all the details of the trip, step by step."

"This is fun," I thought. "Here I am in Cleveland on my way back – but how am I to know that I really am here, now? Oh, well, I'll start over again."

Beginning my mental trip again I meticulously went through each sequence: driving out of Buffalo on Route 20, then on to Cleveland; this time I continued westward to Chicago where I became even more exacting in my details! Up the Outer Drive I went, visualizing every landmark, sign, the traffic, even the view of Lake Michigan as seen from the Drive. Everything down to the finest detail existed in my memory, put there by the hundreds of times I had traveled this route. Finally there I was at the front door of my apartment building on the north side of Chicago!

It was very vivid. I walked to the elevator and paused to decide whether to ride the elevator or run up the short flight of steps. I decided to ride and pushed the button. Getting off the elevator, I walked down the short distance of carpeted hallway to my apartment door. I turned the door handle. Why wasn't it locked?

Entering the apartment, I had the feeling I was expected. But it was only an hour since I had told my wife my return would be delayed another two weeks!

Going through the front room, I glanced at the couch where my son usually slept. He wasn't there! I walked on to the bedroom. The street lights shone into the room from Sheridan Road and I saw clearly the bed where my wife and my daughter were apparently deep asleep. Looking around at the familiar surroundings, the pictures, furniture, etc., I noticed something I seemed to consider unusual – I could see myself in the mirror of the dresser next to the bed! And the lights from Sheridan Road cast my shadow onto the floor and over the bed.

I reached over my daughter, Lisa, and touched my wife gently on the chest.

She reacted instantly! She sat upright and stared directly into my eyes, only inches from her own.

I sensed a great fear. I was picking up her emotions; however, her thoughts were unknown to me. Possibly the fear content of her thoughts blocked their meaning and my understanding.

At that precise instant I was filled with a feeling of "not wanting to frighten." At the same time, I wanted to know the cause of her fear. Then suddenly I was back in my room in the rooming house in Niagara Falls!

I lay on my bed for hours reflecting on the experience. The feeling of fear was still with me as I had sensed it when looking into my wife's eyes after touching her. The experience remained vivid and I reasoned that if it had been just as vivid to Mrs. Otto it surely would have frightened her.

It was dawn before I slept.

Eventually I returned home to Chicago from the east. Neither Mrs. Otto nor I mentioned this experience. I felt if my wife had experienced anything in connection with it she surely would speak of it to me. If she had experienced nothing there was nothing to talk about.

Late in May or early in June we attended a party with a group of friends in Elmwood Park. A guest from New York, Irwin Vaxler, had been doing a great deal of research in the field of psychism and spoke about "teleportation." The subject induced a great deal of discussion and argument to which I listened intently. After a while I decided to tell my story.

"Don't knock it, folks," I said. "Let me tell you of an experience I had a few months ago."

After I had described my experience there was a moment of silence, then everyone started to ask questions at once.

Going over the details again, I stated that I had no way to validate it.

Suddenly, from behind me, my wife spoke abruptly, "Why didn't you tell me you had done that?"

My surprise at her outburst must have been obvious to everyone. Turning to her, I said, "I wasn't sure you had seen me, honey. If you did, why didn't you tell me about it?"

Mrs. Otto said, "You scared me half to death. Why did you punch me so hard on the chest?"

"Punch you?" I exclaimed. "I merely touched you lightly, to wake you."

Our friends were excited. This new development was exciting to me too. My first question was about the substance of the figure my wife had seen. Could she consider it a physical figure of me or was it a wispy, ghost-like entity or merely an image in her mind?

Mrs. Otto answered, "You were there, all right. You leaned across Lisa and poked me real hard on the chest."

"I know that, honey," I said, "but could you see through me or was I solid?"

"As far as I know, you were actually there. I saw you just as I see you now!" she answered.

I asked if there were anything else, any little detail she could remember, but she said, "No, nothing."

Not being entirely satisfied, I asked her to go over the entire experience.

Mrs. Otto stated she first had heard me at the door but could not recall hearing any keys being used. She had heard me whistling a merry tune as I was accustomed to do when returning home. She then heard me walk across the room, pause for a moment (possibly at the couch), and then proceed into the bedroom. All this while, she said, she felt it couldn't be me because she just had spoken with me on the phone and I was in Niagara Falls. She said she had remained quietly in bed and the next thing she recalled was a hard punch on her chest which caused her to sit upright. In terror she had found herself looking right into my eyes, only inches from her own.

I asked her why she was frightened.

She said, "One reads about people seeing a vision of someone. Later they hear that someone has had an accident or something. I thought something had happened to you!"

I asked where our son Jon was that night and after a moment she answered, "He was staying at a friend's home that night."

The talk now became general and our friends asked many pertinent questions about the incident. The main question was about the tangibility of the vision Mrs. Otto had seen. She was firm, however, in claiming that her vision appeared solid indeed since she even could see me reflected in the mirror and that I had cast a shadow which fell across the bed as I leaned over her!

This was extremely interesting to me, of course, because it bore out the details of the trip as I had experienced it. But it leads to an even more important question: could I cast a shadow if I were not there *physically*?

The reality of such an experience is baffling when one speculates on how a body could be transported 500 miles in an instant – and back in another instant. And, if it is not really a physical transportation, what is it?

I will always wonder what would have happened if I had spoken softly to my wife instead of touching (punching!) her. Would she have been frightened? Could we have conversed?

And last but not least, will I have another opportunity to find answers to these questions?

John Otto: Pilot, merchant marine engineer and UFO researcher who experimented with contacting UFOs via powerful radio transmitters.

FATE August 1966

A Case of Teleportation?

John A. Webb

"The ghost came from the other world, but with his own flesh and bones!" writes Don Luis Gonzalez Obregon in his book, *Las Calles de Méjico*.

On the morning of October 25, 1593, he relates, a soldier suddenly appeared in the Plaza Mayor of Mexico City. A soldier dressed in the uniform of the regiment which was at that moment guarding the walled citadel of Manila in the Philippine Islands.

With the soldier's strange appearance came the rumor that His Excellency Gomez Perez Dasmariñas, Governor of the Philippines, was dead. A preposterous rumor, of course! But one that spread through the city like wildfire.

Puzzling as to how the soldier could have traveled more than 9,000 miles without so much as soiling his uniform, the authorities nevertheless jailed him as a deserter from the Philippine regiment.

Weeks passed while the soldier languished in prison; the long, slow weeks necessary for news to travel by sailing ship from the Philippines to Acapulco, then by messenger across the sky-high mountains and down into the valley of Mexico.

Suddenly, Mexico City was quaking with news. His Excellency the Governor of the Philippines was dead; murdered by a mutinous Chinese crew off Punta de Azufre shortly after he had left his island home on a military expedition against the Moluccas! Moreover, he had been murdered on the very day the Philippine soldier had appeared in the plaza of Mexico City.

The Holy Tribunal of the Inquisition took charge of the soldier. He could not tell them how he had been transported from Manila to Mexico. Only that it had been "in less time than it takes a cock to crow." Nor could he tell them how it had come to pass that Mexico City was buzzing with the news of the governor's death even before it was known in Manila.

At the order of the Holy Tribunal, the soldier was returned to the Philippines for further investigation into the mysterious matter. Irrefutable witnesses came forward to swear to the fact that the soldier had been on duty in the island city on the night of October 24. Just as it had been proven beyond doubt that on the following morning he had been apprehended in the plaza of Mexico City, more than 9,000 miles away.

A legend? Not according to the records of the chroniclers of the Order of San Agustin and the Order of Santo Domingo. Not according to Dr. Antonio de Morga, high justice of the criminal court of the Royal Audiencia of New Spain, in his *Sucesos de las Islas Filipinas*.

Is it, then, another authenticated instance of what Charles Fort called teleportation?

FATE May 1949

THE BERMUDA TRIANGLE and DEVIL'S SEA

BERMUDa SHORtCUt

Bruce Gernon

Traveling through time right here on Earth is not only possible – it is a fact, for it happened to me in an aircraft years ago. On the first Friday of December 1970, on our return to Palm Beach, my father and I experienced a flight that we will never forget.

My dad and I had been flying our own plane in the Bahamas since 1967 and had made at least a dozen flights to and from Andros Island. Everything seemed normal on that fateful day in December when my dad and I and Chuck Lafayette, a business associate, lifted off the runway at Andros Town Airport just after 3 PM in a brand-new Beechcraft Bonanza A36.

Shortly after takeoff, I noticed an elliptical cloud directly in front of us about a mile away, hovering only about 500 feet above the ocean. It was a typical lenticular cloud, but I had never seen one that low.

Miami Flight Service reported over the VHF radio that the weather was good, so we continued. But the lenticular cloud quickly changed into a huge cumulus cloud. We were climbing at 1,000 feet per minute, and the cloud seemed to be building up at the same rate.

Unexpectedly, it caught up and engulfed the Bonanza. After 10 minutes of climbing in and out of this cloud, the airplane finally broke free at 11,500 feet and the sky was clear again.

I leveled the Bonanza off and accelerated to its maximum safe cruising speed of 195 miles per hour. When I looked back at the cloud, I was astonished. It now looked like an immense squall, abnormally shaped in the form of a giant semicircle extending around us. Visibility was about 10 miles and the cloud continued beyond my perception, so it must have been more than 20 miles long. After a few minutes I lost sight of it.

Closed circles

Soon we noticed another cloud building directly in front of us, near the Bimini Islands. It looked a great deal like the cloud that we had just left, except that its top was at least 60,000 feet high. When we came within a few miles of it, we saw that it appeared to emanate directly from the surface of the Earth.

Upon entering the cloud, we witnessed an uncanny spectacle. It became dark and black, without rain, and visibility was about four or five miles. There were no lightning bolts, only extraordinarily bright white flashes that would illuminate the entire surrounding area. The deeper we penetrated, the more intense the flashes became, so we made a 135-degree turn to the left and headed due south out of the cloud.

We had been flying for 27 minutes. We thought we might be able to fly around the cloud, but after six or seven miles we saw that it continued in a near-perfect curve to the east. After two more minutes it became apparent that the cloud near Andros and the cloud near Bimini were actually opposite sides of the same ring-shaped body! The cloud must have formed just off of Andros Island and then rapidly spread outward into the shape of a doughnut with a diameter of 30 miles. This seemed impossible, but there was no other explanation. We were trapped inside a billowing prison, with no way under or over it.

Thirteen miles later, I noticed a large U-shaped opening on the west side of the doughnut cloud. I had no choice but to turn and try to exit through the opening. As we approached, we watched the top ends of the U-gap join, forming a hole. The break in the cloud now formed a perfect horizontal tunnel, one mile wide and more than 10 miles long. We could see the clear blue sky on the other side.

We also saw that the tunnel was rapidly shrinking. I increased the engine RPM, bringing our speed to the caution area of 230 miles per hour. When we entered the tunnel, its diameter had narrowed to only 200 feet.

Into the tunnel

I was amazed at what the shaft now looked like. It appeared to be only a mile long instead of 10-plus as I had originally estimated. Light from the afternoon sun shone through the exit hole and made the silky white walls glow. The walls were perfectly round and slowly constricting. All around the edges were small puffs of clouds of a contrasting gray, swirling counterclockwise around the airplane.

We were in the tunnel for only 20 seconds before we emerged from the other end. For about five seconds I had the strange feeling of weightlessness and an increased forward momentum. When I looked back, I gasped to see the tunnel walls collapse and form a slit that slowly rotated clockwise.

All of our electronic and magnetic navigational instruments were malfunctioning. The compass was slowly spinning even as the airplane flew straight. I contacted Miami and told them we were about 45 miles southeast of Bimini, heading east at 10,500 feet. The radar controller replied that he was unable to identify us anywhere in that area.

Something bizarre had happened. Instead of the blue sky we expected, everything was a dull, grayish white haze. Visibility seemed like more than two miles, yet we could not see the ocean, the horizon, or the sky. The air was very stable and there was no lightning or rain. I like to refer to this as an "electronic fog," because it seemed to be what was interfering with our instruments. I had to use my imagination to feel our way west.

We were in the electronic fog for three minutes when the controller radioed that he had identified an airplane directly over Miami Beach, flying due west. I looked at my watch and saw that we had been flying for less than 34 minutes. We could not yet have reached Miami Beach – we should have been approaching the Bimini Islands. I told the controller that he must have identified another airplane and that we were approximately 90 miles southwest of Miami and still looking for Bimini.

Suddenly the fog started breaking apart, in a weird sort of electronic fashion. Long horizontal lines appeared in the fog on either side of us. The lines widened into slits about four or five miles long. We saw blue sky through them. The slits continued expanding and joined together. Within eight seconds, all the slits had joined, and the gray fog had disappeared. All I could see was brilliant blue sky as my pupils adjusted to the abrupt increase in brightness. Then, I saw the barrier island of Miami Beach directly below.

You do the math

After we landed at Palm Beach I realized that the flight had taken a little less than 47 minutes. I thought something must have been wrong with the airplane's timer, yet all three of our watches showed that it was 3:48 PM.

I had never made it from Andros to Palm Beach in less than 75 minutes, even on a direct route. Our course on this flight was quite indirect and probably covered close to 250 miles. How could the airplane travel 250 miles in 47 minutes? We taxied to customs, ending the fortuitous flight. We didn't talk about it for a long time.

I could not logically understand what had happened during that flight, although I felt it was significant and reviewed it in my mind several times a day. In 1972 I heard about the so-called Bermuda Triangle and disappearances of boats and airplanes because of a possible time warp. It was then that I realized that time itself was the key.

It should have taken about four minutes to travel through the tunnel, since it appeared to be between 10 and 15 miles long. Instead, this is precisely how long it took for us to leave the storm and reach clear skies. The remarkable thing is that we did not come out of the storm 90 miles away from Miami as we should have. Somehow, we skipped through 90 miles of space.

Time and space cannot be separated because they are one and the same. Today, time travel is a theoretical possibility. My flight showed that it is a fact. When my airplane entered the tunnel, I saw time physically change. The gigantic slits that appeared three minutes later were the exit of the time tunnel vortex. We had traveled through 100 miles of space and 30 minutes of time – in a little more than three minutes.

Bruce Gernon: Aviator and author. His 1970 experience is one of the classic Bermuda Triangle cases, told for the first time in his own words in FATE.

FATE September 1998

THE TRIANGLE WITH FOUR (OR MORE) SIDES

Martin S. Caidin

Bermuda Triangle

It all depends upon what you're reading. Sometimes it's called the Bermuda Triangle. But if the writer selects on the basis of a more commanding and grisly effect, the words shift to become the Devil's Triangle. It's also known as the Devil's Graveyard and a host of other titles, which mercifully we will put aside.

All the names point to that area of the Atlantic Ocean infamous for a staggering loss – often without any trace – of ships, planes and people. Most books and articles on the Bermuda Triangle (the name may be less esoteric but at least we're not pounding it for effect) are inordinately fond of reproducing a map, or perhaps a satellite photo of that ocean area, with a dramatically heavy line that runs from the island of Bermuda straight down to Key West, doodles off to somewhere in Cuba or Puerto Rico, and then shoots back northward to Bermuda.

But that's *not* the way it is. Oh, there's a specific area, all right, but it's difficult to find more than a few people who will agree on just what is that area. Even those of us who've flown through the Bermuda Triangle, and sailed it as well, find it necessary at times to alter the sides of the "Triangle" because of some new event or disappearance that adds another bit of hard data to the legend.

We're talking about a half-million square miles of ocean that's a trapezium – a rectangle in which no two sides or angles are the same. It's a skewed rectangle, and it derives its ominous reputation from hard numbers.

1,700 vanished

In the 30 years from 1945 through 1975, 67 ships and boats of all sizes, and at least 192 aircraft (there are more but exact proof is lacking) of all types, involving approximately 1,700 human beings, have vanished within the Bermuda Triangle without a shred of evidence to explain their loss.

Not a word of what you have just read is conjecture, or bending a single fact, or assuming anything. It is simply the truth, a bitter and often frightening reality. The why of those disappearances is where the shouting and name-calling begins, but, hold on just a moment until we better define what this writer, pilot and seaman defines a bit more carefully as the "Triangle."

Dimensions

Convenient as it may be to start defining the area by stabbing a pencil on the chart dot called Bermuda, that would be too specific without justification. Take the area of Bermuda, one or two hundred miles in all directions from that island (and other smaller islands), and then draw a wide band to Wilmington/North Myrtle Beach in North Carolina. From this area, make another wide swath generally southward, but taking in the entire coastline right on down to an area perhaps a hundred miles south of Key West. Continue southeast, still with that wide swath, to Puerto Rico, and then bend around to a generally northeast direction back to Bermuda. You may have a rectangle with four unequal sides or something that seems to have five sides, but you're just as accurate if you draw on that chart a huge lopsided ink blot that takes in the same general area.

I've taken this time for specifying the area itself to avoid the urge of so many to create a charted triangle to lend credence to the shape. The shape doesn't mean a thing; it's the area within from which ships

Shaded area marks the general Bermuda "Triangle"

and planes have vanished without leaving any sign of what caused them to disappear. If you utilize this shape and area, then you'll discover the 67 ships and 192 planes are somewhat fewer than the actual number of disappearances. In any attempt to learn what caused these mysterious and frustrating losses of ships, aircraft and people, there's a natural, almost urgent, need to blame the shape of the area involved, and that is extremely misleading. It doesn't supply any answers, and to be blunt about it – you're dealing with a cop-out. Questions with possible answers, but to date nothing specific.

Many disappearances

I stated that the 67 ships and 192 aircraft are not the total number. Many aircraft flying along the American East Coast or down through the islands that take us, in our "chart swath," to Puerto Rico before bending northeast back to Bermuda have never gone into the record books. Pilots often fly into this area without filing a flight plan or leaving any other

205

evidence of their intended route. Others get caught in weather and end up far from shore in the Triangle.

Many military aircraft on missions, for one reason or another that have been classified, are never identified. You can count on perhaps hundreds or even thousands of foreigners, the drug runners, the illegal entry of aliens, the gun runners, the escapees from many island countries trying to reach the American mainland who have sailed or flown to nameless oblivion in this area.

Before we can understand how and why there has been such a stupendous loss of life without even a trace of such loss, let me make a point that in the name of accuracy and common sense requires unquestioned statement. Many thousands of sea voyages have been made through the Bermuda Triangle in absolute safety, peace and harmony – and you can add whatever adjectives you wish to those trips.

Just as there have been hundreds of thousands of flights of aircraft through the Triangle without even the cough of an engine or the unexplained twitch of an instrument dial. That issue must be stated clearly, lest the reader judge that launching into the Triangle assures one of fright or mystery "just because you're there." After all, airliners have been flying through that area for decades in absolute safety.

But not all of them, and that also is the issue at hand. The loss of several hundred ships and aircraft is no small matter, and one must be weighed against the other.

Qualifications

For the record, and that is important for the reader, I've been flying in the area we identify as the Bermuda Triangle for decades. Literally. This includes aircraft beginning with the diminutive Piper TriPacer and Cessna 172, and then scaling upward to the Piper Apache, Piper Aztec, Beech Twin Bonanza (I ran a small charter airline with a few of these operating out of Florida), Cessna 310, Piper Comanche and Twin Comanche, the Douglas C-47 and its civilian equal, the DC-3. I've gone through this same area in the Douglas C-118 (military version of the OC-6B), the Lockheed C-130 Hercules, the Consolidated PBY-6A Catalina and, well, there are others, but I believe the point is made. I've made the flights in perfect weather (severe clear) and I've been out there in a violent hurricane, on a search mission for a downed airliner (at least we judge it was downed; it vanished with all aboard).

Our interest is not with the flights made without incident, for those are like any other flights to other destinations. Nor am I going to refer to the flights of pilot friends who went through eerie and frightening moments and were deeply grateful for surviving a flight they believed was their last. As sincere and accurate though such flights may be, that is secondary information, and our concern is with firsthand experience. No intermediaries.

Real incident
The incident at hand is real, detailed, recorded, witnessed and established beyond even the most tenuous shred of doubt. There may be, and likely there will be, naysayers in the reading audience. Little matter. This is a moment of reality and it matters not one whit what somebody *who wasn't there* may have in the way of comment. At its best, it is armchair pontificating; at worst it's just someone babbling about something about which they know next to nothing.

June 11, 1986
The aircraft is a Consolidated PBY-6A Catalina; this particular model was manufactured under license in Canada. It is a large flying boat that performed yeoman service before, during and after World War II. This particular "Cat" is the property of Connie Edwards of Big Spring, Texas, and carries the FAA identification (registration) of N4C.

On the 11th of June 1986, we neared the conclusion of a flight that had taken the flying boat from Texas into Canada, to and through the Azores, into Lisbon, Portugal, then northward to Santiago, Spain, and farther northward to land in Plymouth Harbor in southern England. Later we flew on to Yeovilton, the British base for its Fleet Air Arm, before starting the return flight from England back to the Azores, and then a flight (into strong headwinds) from Lajes in the Azores to Bermuda that took us more than 22 hours of nonstop flying.

Our last leg – of mine and my wife, Dee Dee, who is also a pilot – was from Bermuda to Jacksonville (JAX) Naval Air Station on the northeast coastline of Florida. Among the people in the Catalina for this run were myself and Dee Dee; Connie Edwards of incredible flying experience and skill; Randy Sohn, an airline captain who also is qualified to fly *any* piston-engine warbird built anywhere in the world; USN Captain Art Ward, probably the leading instrument pilot of the

The PBY-6A Catalina at the Jacksonville, Florida Naval Station just after Martin S. Caidin and his party flew through the Bermuda Triangle

entire US Navy; Al Brown, veteran Air Force flight engineer, mechanic and pilot; and, the youngest of the lot, Connie's son, Tex Edwards, who in his teens was rated for everything from single-engine planes to four-engine transports or bombers. Understand the importance of these names; veteran, experienced, skilled, ability-recognized pilots who'd flown through, over and around most of the world.

Just as germane to the flight were the instrumentation and avionics (flight electronics) we had aboard this airplane. We're talking about a considerable fortune in equipment. Aside from the two-of-everything of instruments, Connie and Al Brown packed into this airplane a radar altimeter, an HF radio, VLF Omega and other navigational equipment. *Then* they added more radios and navigation gear, including a second Loran C (device to pinpoint locations using information from overhead satellites), two more ADFs, another encoding altimeter and – well, put it this way: our radar altimeters measured the waves beneath us down to the accuracy of *one foot.* Our navigation systems would let us

208

know – anywhere in the world – if we were so much as a tenth of a mile off the planned course.

We communicated by satellite links with any spot in the world. We had a system that let us link up to a weather satcom at 22,300 miles so that we were fed printouts of photographs taken from space of where we were flying at that moment, and you can't get better weather checking than that!

We had equipment in that airplane that not too many years before this flight was a dream – not yet available – for pilots. We also had more powerful engines that went into this bird, and we had two huge fuel tanks slung beneath the wings (longer than the wings of a B-17 bomber) so that we could fly at least 28 to 30 hours nonstop.

We enjoyed the satellite photo printouts. They showed the only clouds far south of us, a line that curved southward and then westward from Bermuda to the Melbourne area. The nearest clouds to us once we were on our way would be at least 200 miles south of us.

Into the milk bottle

On the morning of June 11, 1986, in perfect, warm, balmy weather, we set course for JAX Naval Air Station. You could see just about forever. Few flights were set up as well as this with the skies severe clear, two purring powerful engines, a grand flying machine with great inherent stability, the safety of being able to land on the ocean if that ever became our need, and an array of electronics that gave us a running account of our position about as close as you can get to a gnat's eyelash.

Beautiful; that was the word.

Those pilots who decided to "sit this one out" and let the others fly gathered in the aft compartment between the two big gun blisters where leather couches and pillows had replaced the .50 caliber machine guns. After a few hours in the air, my wife went forward to take the left seat – the position for pilot-in-command. It was great hand-flying, which means you *had* to fly hands-on. Despite all the super electronic gizmos on board, the PBY didn't have an autopilot, which is just the way Connie Edwards wanted his airplane. You were up there to *fly*. But it was calm flying. Pay attention to where the needles and numbers on the gauges pointed and fly her with a gentle hand. The PBY is like a whale, and everything seems to take place in slow motion.

Disappearing wing

Then, it happened. I was up front in the cockpit, standing behind and between the two pilot seats. I watched idly through the side windows at groups of dolphins beneath us, and every now and then we'd pass a sailing ship or a sea-going yacht. I shifted my gaze from the right side of the airplane to the left, and had the left wing, all the way out to the wing-tip (wingspan is 110 feet), in sight.

It disappeared. I blinked. Nothing seemed to have changed. The engines thundered smoothly, the propellers synchronized, the great flying boat steady as a rock. But I couldn't see the outer portion of the left wing. A pilot's first thought, of course, is that we'd flown into a cloud, or a fog, or even some crazy mist that was heaving up to 4,000 feet. But a few moments before moving forward to the cockpit I had checked the metsat photos beamed down from space, and there wasn't a smidgen of cloud or anything else within 200 miles of us.

I turned to look at the right wing, and in that movement my vision moved through the field of view of the cockpit looking forward. I saw the nose clearly and remembered how starkly the cleat in the nose center (for mooring) stood out clearly. Beyond the airplane nose there was nothing.

What in the hell was this? I snapped a look out to the right window – and the right wing simply disappeared from sight! It was an eerie feeling, as though we'd flown into some impossible limbo. I took careful stock of everything about me, and then noticed that what had been blue sky had also changed color. A creamy yellow, as though we were in the middle of a bottle of eggnog. I looked around in all directions.

We seemed to be suspended in an infinity of murky yellow. If we couldn't check the instruments, there was no way to know we were flying at just over 100 miles per hour – as we saw on the ASI (air-speed indicator). And looking at the instrument panel was enough to chill anyone's blood down to the freezing level.

Failed instruments

A pilot depends upon his (or her) instruments for balance, maneuvering, and navigation when you're flying in IMC (Instrument Meteorological Conditions), and sure as winter follows summer we were IMC! But the instruments so important to us were going crazy – and few things will raise the hackles along the back of your neck than the sight of those gauges and instruments going belly up.

Because there wasn't any more hint of why they were failing than there was for the world outside the airplane to dissolve into that creamy yellow murk. What was strange became stranger. We looked in every direction from the airplane.

We were surprised to see we had a narrow-diameter "hole" through which we could look straight up to see blue sky, and, if we looked straight down, through this same small-diameter space, there was the ocean. It was as if a long pipe extended from the surface to the sky above, providing this keyhole of vision, and the pipe sped along with the airplane.

Our gauges belly up

The first sign of something wrong with the gauges was picked up by Dee Dee, since she was in the left seat and scanning the gauges as part of her flying. We didn't need the magnetic compass with all our super avionics, but the thing is supposed to perform in a reliable manner. Ours began to swing back and forth and quickly went into a blur of movement as it whirled crazily in its bath of alcohol.

Moments later the DG (the Directional Gyro that supplies a gyroscopic heading to follow) played catchup with the mag compass and began its own wild (and useless) swinging. As fast as we could move our gaze from one instrument to another, they were failing. The artificial horizon – a gyroscopic representation of the horizon and the world outside the airplane – fell over like a punctured chicken and wobbled as if demented.

And then the real trouble started. We had a zillion-bucks worth of super electronics in this airplane, and abruptly they began to fall over as if paralyzed. Two million dollars of avionics just up and died. We didn't know what in the hell was wrong other than just about everything in that airplane save the barometric pressure gauges were gone. The LORAN was useless. Even the electronic fuel gauges, showing rate of flow and quantity, fluttered and blinked and became erratic, which is the same as worthless. Our intricate navigation gear blinked a few times and then every dial read 8888888888. Then the radios went dead!

Now, everything electronic was still being fed power from the aircraft electrical system. All power flow was normal, but none of it worked anymore. It was as if everything electronic had gone into a coma. We couldn't see even the wingtips, we had no navigation, the most rudimentary of gauges – the mag compass – had become a whirling dervish, and Dee Dee continued to fly by "aiming" at the brightest area of the horizon, which meant westward. We took turns in the right seat or standing behind the pilot seats, "riding shotgun" on each other.

We were flying now by the most rudimentary systems – airspeed, altitude, rate of climb or descent, and a turn-slip-skid indicator that operated like a seal balancing a ball on its nose and functioned without outside power, and that was it. This was the way pilots flew only a dozen years after the Wright Brothers took to the air!

Plane flew perfectly

But that's all we had. We had no idea of what had cut our equipment down to junk. The engines roared perfectly, the airplane flew with that solid Catalina feel, but we were no longer in any world we knew. We figured if it was crazy up high, let's go down by studying the waves through that peephole of looking straight down, and also counting (but not too much) on the altimeter.

We dropped down to perhaps 20 or 30 feet off the water, but we couldn't see forward any distance greater than that. "We're gonna run into a damn ship down this low," someone offered, and immediately we went back to altitude.

Still that same gummy, yellow gunk all about us. If I ever wanted to know what it's like to drift through limbo where the dominant hue is creamy eggnog, I've now experienced this.

After a while, out of touch with the rest of the planet, we began exchanging pilots in the left seat. Young Tex took over for a while and Art Ward stayed up front with him, with Al Brown studying everything from behind them.

I wasn't flying this leg, so I went back with Dee Dee to the gun blisters where we might as well have been in some luxury salon. That was another crazy part about all this. No matter that what we were in – trapped is as good a word as any – no one in the airplane reacted as if there were any danger. Hell, with two exceptions (Dee Dee and Tex), the rest of us had been flying all our lives and we'd had a few memorable experiences. The calm of the pilots would have astounded anyone not familiar with this background. We were here, it was impossible, the airplane was still flying, so, keep flying.

212

Connie Edwards and Randy Sohn went forward to take the controls. About 90 minutes (estimated by clock time) out of JAX, we seemed to penetrate an invisible curtain. Imagine you're up there in this soup with us. For hours the only world is eggnog and that ridiculous periscope view of straight up or down, and the most advanced flight electronic systems in the world are as dead as dodos.

Then suddenly you're flying in perfect, crystal-clean, clear air. No more eggnog. We swung into a wide turn to see where we had been. The sky was absolutely clear behind us as far as we could see. Whatever had enveloped us for hours was gone.

"Hey, we're coming back on line!" came the word. The artificial horizon revived itself, the directional gyro steadied down and the mag compass quivered gently. The rows of 8888888888 blurred away and the proper numbers began to read out on radio, LORAN, transponder, radar altimeter and everything else. We could talk via satcom link to anywhere in the world. The ocean was clear beneath us, the sky above a bright blue. We passed an increasing number of ships, made contact with JAX NAS, saw we'd have to punch through some heavy rain showers (and they looked *wonderful*). Connie set her down on the JAX runway like we had feathers beneath us.

For some four hours, what happened to us, as any sober scientist or engineer will tell you without a moment's hesitation, was and is absolutely impossible.

Invisible genie

Of course, those scientists weren't up there with us, and so no matter how many sheepskins hang on their walls, they don't know what the hell they're talking about.

Let me conclude this with the wisdom of a great pilot and a great writer recently departed from this life, for no one ever said it better than did Ernest K. Gann in his magnificent book, *Fate Is the Hunter*.

He said that no matter what the science or the engineering, no matter how thorough the planning, no matter how skilled the crews or exhaustive the preparations, airplanes will go down from causes unknown. And a pilot unskilled in instrument flight on this day of the yellow sky would never have survived those hours of limbo.

"Somewhere in the heavens," wrote Ernie Gann, *"there is a great invisible genie who every so often lets down his pants and pisses all over the pillars of science."*

Any explanation?

No one has ever come forward with an acceptable explanation of the "yellow sky, as if flying in a bottle of eggnog," or how it suddenly appeared, or what it was. Neither is there any clear-cut definition of why gyroscopic and magnetic instruments, which had worked perfectly for weeks of flying, suddenly spun uselessly. And there is even greater mystery as to why several million dollars' worth of new electronics – always with power fed properly to them – became useless and ceased to function.

The single explanation that appears to make sense is that the Catalina flying boat was enveloped, or was affected by, an intense electromagnetic field that dumped the instruments and "blanked out" the electronic equipment. Where did it come from? No one knows. Or was it really an electromagnetic field? No one knows that either. But the point was made that any pilot caught in that "soup" who lacked experienced flying skills with basic instruments and no outside reference would almost certainly have lost control and crashed into the ocean.

We add this item to this report. The erratic behavior of magnetic and gyroscopic instruments is uncommon, but it has been encountered by other aircraft and pilots. So has the "yellow sky" where all reference to the outside world vanishes.

The more experienced pilots have emerged from their travail.

But not all, and we don't know how many fell victim to these bizarre conditions.

Martin S. Caidin (1927-1997): Authority in science, aviation, crime, oceanography and the military; pilot, flight chaplain, Federal Aviation Administration examiner, deputy sheriff, undercover agent, news reporter and broadcaster, race car driver and teacher, among other vocations. Author of more than 140 books.

FATE January 1993

Eyewitness in the Bermuda Triangle

John Miller

Here the vast bed of the waters, seamed and scarred into a thousand conflicting channels, burst suddenly into frenzied convulsion – heaving, boiling, hissing – gyrating in gigantic and innumerable vortices and all whirling and plunging on to eastward with a rapidity which water never elsewhere assumes, except in precipitous descents.

From *A Descent into the Maelstrom*,
by Edgar Allen Poe

Up close and personal

Many investigators have written about the Bermuda Triangle from afar, but no description of that most enigmatic area of ocean can match the accounts of people who have actually lived there. One such person is Andy Raymond, a Chicago contract engineer, who made the Bermuda Triangle his home from 1979 to 1982. During that time, he was project manager for the "Island of Science," where professionally trained researchers experimented with solar power, the nutritional potential of seaweed and an accelerated wind lab.

Under his direction were 40 Bahamians and a dozen Haitians, who commuted daily from other nearby islands, while he resided on the Island of Science, with occasional flights to Great Harbour Cay, about 30 minutes away.

No nonsense guy

It was on these air commutes that the Bermuda Triangle phenomena would often occur. Most of Raymond's flights from the Island of Science were strictly routine, but during a few of them his magnetic compass would spin crazily, as though powered by an electric motor. For a man like Andy Raymond, such occurrences had to be the results of presently unknown but ultimately explainable natural forces.

He was familiar with most of the paranormal theories and stories about the Bermuda Triangle and dismissed them all out of hand as just plain malarkey. He is a no-nonsense construction engineer who knows how to party hearty with no room in between for wacko speculations. But one flight in particular was to open his mind and shake any rational explanation for unusual happenings in the Devil's Triangle.

July 5th, 1980, a date he will remember the rest of his life, began usual enough. It was one of those picture-postcard perfect days in south coastal Florida, with the sun shining out of an unobstructed sky on a mirror-smooth sea. Andy was along for a ride with his old friend, Howard Smith, a highly experienced bush pilot, who was returning a repaired clutch plate for a boat with motor problems in Great Harbour Cay, 70 nautical miles away.

Smith's single-engine Cessna 172, call letters 7-9-Tango, was loaded with some of the most advanced instrumentation available to civilian aviators. He had a costly DME (distance measuring equipment, a sophisticated device for measuring the relationship of time and distance in flight), the latest in radio-direction finders, electric and magnetic compasses and a transponder. They arrived in Bimini without incident by noon, had a leisurely lunch, then took off into the same pristine weather conditions for Little Stirrup Cay, northernmost of the Bahamas and hardly more than an hour away.

Sudden clouds

Not long into their flight, however, they ran into a thick cloud cover and the sky grew suddenly dark. The array of instruments functioned perfectly. Both Smith and Andy had made this hop numerous times before, so neither had cause for concern, despite flying blind through the overcast.

When their DME informed them that they had reached their destination, they dropped beneath the cloud cover to initiate their landing approach, but the scene that spread out before them belonged to another world or some alternate reality. Little Stirrup Cay was nowhere to be seen. Nor was there a sign of land anywhere in the otherwise island-bedecked part of the sea. No less awful was the eerie appearance of the water below them.

Boiling copper water

"It looked just like boiling copper," Andy recalled. "I have seen every kind of light effect the sun can bounce off the surface, but never anything even remotely approaching this." Moreover, the sun was hidden behind the thick overcast, while the waves roiled as though heated by some impossible, submarine furnace. They glistened in a golden red fire that appeared to be generated from *within* the sea.

Smith got on the horn to Fort Lauderdale for assistance. The radio was dead. Flying too low now, he ascended into the darkening cloud cover again, trusting to his instruments. Now they both could feel a strange tingling of electricity in the air. Moments later, the little Cessna suddenly plummeted 500 feet before Smith could restore control. Known as "micro-bursts" of air, they are powerful down-drafts within storm clouds. After the third or fourth occurrence, they descended beneath the clouds once more. The evil-looking, copper-colored sea was gone, the sky suddenly cleared and before them was another private aircraft.

They followed it for a few minutes as it led them in a final approach to Great Harbour Cay, their point of origin. Incredibly, they were back where they started, even though they flew in a *straight line in the opposite direction.*

With the exception of their radio, the instruments had operated perfectly. Later, Smith calculated the time aloft to the distance covered and deduced that it would have been impossible to go out over open water as far as they did and round trip it back to Great Harbour Cay.

Afterward, Andy learned of firsthand accounts from friends in the US Navy and Coast Guard of numerous, inexplicable disappearances made more mysterious by the fact that the area defined as the Bermuda Triangle is among the most thoroughly monitored quadrants on the globe. It is constantly eavesdropped by the Bahama Air Service and Rescue, together with military and civilian radar and radio operators.

Theoretically, no serious trouble should occur without somebody taking notice. Andy himself survived two separate shipwrecks in the Bermuda Triangle and was rescued before he had a chance to get wet.

Baffling tragedy

In the fall of 1981, he was involved in a baffling tragedy that still haunts him. It concerned two lifelong, robust friends in their 60s, who had grown up together in the Bahamas and understood those waters better than almost anyone. Their sailing expertise was well known, so when they filed their float plan to West Palm Beach, no one doubted they could make the entirely routine cruise in under six hours. Even so, they were in regular ship-to-shore radio contact with their wives back at Grand Harbour Cay. They broadcast their position every 30 minutes on a high-powered, single-band transmitter. The two old sea hands cast off at 9 AM under a windless, cloudless sky across a glass-smooth sea.

As promised, they radioed their precise location every half hour, describing the conditions through which they sailed as ideal. But when they failed to make their 1 PM transmission, their wives alerted the authorities. Within minutes, an armada of private, Coast Guard and B.A.S.R. boats, including Andy Raymond, and a squadron of search aircraft, swept the placid waters in all directions in a 200-mile radius of the 58-foot-*Hattaris* yacht's last known position. The intensive search went on after nightfall and all the next day. Search efforts continued for another week before being called off. During all that time, the sea remained innocently calm. But it bore not a single trace of the vanished boat or its two accomplished seamen.

Not even an oil slick

No oil slick, not even a single seat cushion – absolutely nothing was left behind. "I have seen all kinds of vessels, large and small, go down," Andy said. "Without exception, they all leave massive amounts of debris which survive their sinking by days. You would not believe the masses of material that cover the seas after a wreck. Even the smallest yacht belches enormous clouds of oil long after sinking. For a boat as big as the craft they sailed to go down and leave neither a huge oil slick nor a carpet of floating debris is impossible, especially considering the calm condition of the sea at that time."

Blue Holes

Some days after the unsolved disappearance, Andy saw what he felt might be a clue to the deadly mystery of the Bermuda Triangle. While walking along the beach in water up to his knees, he came upon one of the Bahamas' famous "Blue Holes." These represent a phenomenon not yet understood by oceanographers, but are still being researched as the strangest feature of the Caribbean. They vary in diameter from a few feet to perhaps hundreds of yards, occur in shallow depths, contain water of a remarkably light blue color and go down, straight as a shaft, to immeasurable depths.

Exploring a Blue Hole about 10 years ago, Jacques Cousteau photographed a perfectly preserved, turn-of-the-century rowboat sitting on a shelf about 80 feet down, as though carefully placed there by some mermaid who collected antique vessels.

Andy speculates these Blue Holes may go down to the very floor of the sea, where submarine earthquakes surge water pressure through them to generate sudden vortices. Appearing without warning for brief periods, they resemble a whirlpool like that created when the plug is pulled from a bathtub of water. The force they exert on the surface of the water is so great that anything within its vicinity is sucked without a trace to the bottom of the ocean, including aircraft, which are pulled into the vortex by down drafts similar to the micro-bursts Andy and Howard experienced in 1980. The atmospheric disturbances caused by such a vortex could account for the electromagnetic anomalies encountered in the immediate area of a disappearance.

Whatever the source of those disappearances, Andy Raymond will never forget his three years in the Bermuda Triangle. He needs no one to convince him of its terrible mystery, because he knows it is *real*.

FATE January 1993

THE DEVIL'S SEA: ANOTHER BERMUDA TRIANGLE?

Barbara J. Bigham

For more than a century scientists and researchers have been trying to unravel the mystery of the Bermuda Triangle, that area off the east coast of the United States that has claimed dozens of ships and airplanes and hundreds of human lives. Yet, while our attention remains on this section of our earth, another area continues to gobble up ships and baffle researchers. For the Bermuda Triangle is not unique; across the globe is its partner-in-death, the Devil's Sea.

About 250 miles southeast of the Japanese Island of Honshu, between Iwo Jima and Marcus Island, is an area of turbulent ocean that has become infamous not only because of its natural dangers but because of the mysterious disappearances that have occurred there. Roughly triangular in shape, its general area can be traced between Japan, Guam and the Philippine Islands.

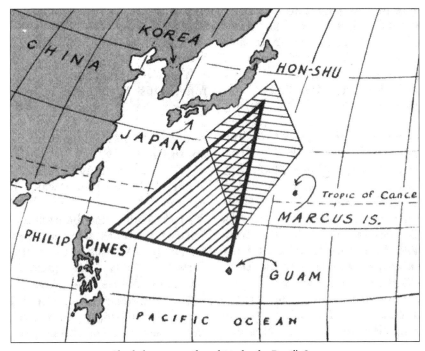

Shaded areas are thought to be the Devil's Sea

A glance at an oceanic map shows this part of the Pacific is scarred by deep trenches and mountainous ridges including the Mariana Trench and the South Honshu Ridge. These oceanic features create violent sea storms, giant tidal waves, whirlpools and underwater volcanoes. Naturally enough, Japanese seamen long have regarded the area as an evil place. Stories of incredible sea monsters that swallow ships whole and leave no trace of their victims have been part of their folklore for 100 years.

Nor were these Japanese seamen naive landlubbers who blamed every sunken ship on sea serpents or evil spirits. They were sea wise sailors, aware of the treachery of the ocean and knowing the disastrous effects the frequent violent storms and rough seas had on their small crafts. Yet the stories continued, many telling of strange disappearances in calm seas with no mention of storms or anything else that could logically account for the ship's loss. In times past, what besides sea monsters could these seamen blame for the mysterious tragedies?

In more modern days these stories of vanished ships have been shrugged off as legends or at most the results of storms on poorly built fishing vessels. But the art of shipbuilding progressed, and the loss of a ship no longer could be brushed off as the inevitable result of rough seas. When modern cruisers, freighters and steamships, built to withstand ocean storms and rough weather, vanished, the world took note.

If only one ship had vanished, the area never would have gained its terrifying reputation, but one after another, with frightening frequency, ships have entered the Devil's Sea and never returned – often during calm weather without a trace of oceanic or atmospheric disturbance.

Shortly after World War II a series of these mysterious disasters rocked the world. No longer could the legends of a "devil's sea" be ignored. Within four years, from 1950 to 1954, at least nine ships were lost in the Devil's Sea area – all without warning, apparent cause or trace. *The New York Times* referred to the Devil's Sea as the "mystery graveyard of nine ships in the last five years," and I have found three specific reports:

- On September 22, 1950, 80 persons were reported missing on a Japanese ship which was headed for Japan. The article notes that searchers "found no trace" of the unnamed vessel.

- On February 23, 1953, a 144-ton fishing vessel, *Azume Maru*, with a crew of 47, was reported missing without a trace after an extensive search 240 miles off the coast of Central Honshu.

- On August 1, 1953, the *Times* reported that ships and planes had searched over 60,000 square miles of the Pacific Ocean for the motor vessel *Venus,* which had sailed for Guam and vanished on July 23, 1953, with 21 persons aboard.

Whatever happened to these nine ships must have happened quickly, for only one was able to send a radio message. Even that cry of distress shed no light on the mystery, for it consisted of one word only: "sinking." Then all contact was lost forever.

After each disappearance, intensive searches scoured the area but, in all cases, not one single survivor, body, life jacket or piece of debris was found.

The Japanese government became increasingly alarmed at the losses and commissioned research teams of scientists from the Tokyo University of Fisheries and Earthquakes, the Research Institute of Tokyo University, and the Tokyo Science Museum to explore the area, to survey weather and water conditions looking for a clue to the phenomena. However, little was learned on the expedition; a new underwater volcano was located but nothing was discovered to explain the disappearance of the nine ships.

Remember, these nine cases include only total, unexplained disappearances. There were other sea disasters in the area during the period, such as the loss of the survey ship *Kaiyo Maru* in 1952. The complete destruction of this ship was found to have been caused by an underwater volcanic explosion off the Myojin Reef. But, as in almost all natural sea disasters – and unlike the total disappearances – enough wreckage was found by searchers to allow for an investigation and determination of the cause of the tragedy.

Even while the research expedition continued another tragedy was added to the list. One of the research vessels, the *Shinyo Maru*, was surveying in the area when radio contact with her was lost. A frantic search turned up nothing; she had vanished like the other ships, another victim of the Devil's Sea.

The New York Times for January 16, 1953, reported:

> *The ship vanished in the same perfect weather that had marked the previous disappearances. Contact was lost with the ship as it reached an area about 70 miles off Japan's east coast, where nine other ships and 215 men have been lost. Only one of the ships – a fishery patrol vessel that was the third to disappear – left any trace of wreckage or bodies. Fear struck through every nearby Japanese fishing village when it was known that the 144-ton Shinyo Maru was missing. Fishermen spoke of a "devil" lurking off the shore. Coast Guard authorities have designated the area a "special danger zone."*

Finally, the Japanese government admitted their consternation and proclaimed the area a "danger zone." For two years the area remained relatively quiet but in March 1957 disaster struck again. In that one month there were six major air accidents in various parts of the world. That in itself is an astounding number and prompted aviators to call it the "nightmare month," but three of them occurred in the Devil's Sea area and were total disappearances.

Until then the Devil's Sea had seemed to be the particular nemesis of seagoing vessels; now suddenly researchers realized that whatever was happening in the area was not solely an ocean-related phenomenon, for aircraft were not safe there either. Within 10 days during March 1957 three United States military planes vanished over the area without a trace.

On March 12 an air force tanker with eight crewmen disappeared between Japan and Wake Island. On March 16 a navy plane carrying five crew members vanished between Japan and Okinawa. Then, on March 22, one of the largest aircraft to be claimed by the area met its tragic fate while en route from Travis Air Force Base to Japan. A military transport with 67 persons on board vanished about 250 miles from Japan. For more than a week a gigantic air-sea search continued but as in previous cases, no wreckage, survivors, bodies or debris were found. *The New York Times* reported on March 23:

> An all-night air search failed to find a trace of the huge, four-engine transport that disappeared as it was nearing the Japanese coast on a routine flight from Travis Air Force Base in California.
>
> Seventy planes and a fleet of naval and fishing vessels combed 75,000 square miles of the Pacific in the second day of one of the biggest searches in US Air Force history.
>
> . The passengers originally were to have flown in another plane which developed minor maintenance problems prior to take off. The ill-fated plane was substituted.
>
> The plane made a stop at Wake Island en route, and the pilot reported at 12:45 AM yesterday…only 90 minutes and 250 miles away from its Tokyo destination.

> *The message was a "normal report" saying the transport was in "A-1 condition."*

Yet that transport was never seen nor heard from again. Not even an oil slick marked its grave.

Since then planes have continued to go missing in the area, especially those traveling from Japan to Guam on a route that crosses the Devil's Sea.

Other flights that have made it to their destination have reported disrupted flights or impossibly high winds. Ivan Sanderson, in his *Invisible Residents*, cited two instances of such disrupted flights. In both cases the aircraft seemingly were caught in winds of extraordinary velocities.

One crew, in a BOAC four engine prop aircraft, reported readings of ground speeds of 550 knots! This would mean a wind of 365 knots. The other case, reported by a retired air force lieutenant colonel who was head navigator aboard a C-97 traveling to Guam from a Pacific island, also involved incredibly high winds. Readings that were checked and rechecked indicated that in one hour the plane apparently had gone 340 nautical miles. Yet when they landed they were told that no unusual winds had been logged by any weather station.

Although Sanderson acknowledged the authenticity of these and similar reports, he questioned whether the actual cause of the unusual readings was high winds.

"The alternative," he wrote, "is that the planes ran into a local *time* (italics his) anomaly, rather than into incredible, undetected and seemingly impossible winds."

Sanderson suggested that such local time anomalies are pockets in space where time runs slower or faster than normal measurement standards. For instance, if a plane slipped into an area in which time runs slower, that plane would have a comparatively longer time to travel farther and thus arrive early. The only known phenomena that can create this effect naturally would be incredibly fast tail winds. If the planes ran into a faster time slot they would move as in slow motion and arrive late, with only impossibly fast head winds as a stated cause. Sanderson admitted to being unable to find a cause for these anomalies or even whether they are the result of an intelligent force.

"To put it simply," Sanderson explained, "the planes 'appeared' to get to their destinations much faster than they should have, according to their maximum speed abilities...yet the only known possible cause would be excessively high velocity winds."

As ships and planes continued to disappear, other theories were developed to explain the phenomena. The United States takes the official stand that these are natural tragedies which have no mysterious overtones.

"Mysterious, mystic, supernatural – unlikely!" a US Coast Guard news release stated on November 23, 1971. "The Coast Guard feels there is nothing mysterious about disappearances in this particular section of the ocean; weather conditions, equipment failure and human error, not something from the supernatural, are what has caused the tragedies."

Although this statement was released in regard to the Bermuda Triangle, the Coast Guard takes the same attitude toward the Devil's Sea.

It is easy to understand why the government refuses to admit that in these sections of the ocean something is happening that cannot be explained by the scientific knowledge we presently possess. When publicity about the Bermuda Triangle disappearances became widespread, thousands of frightened tourists and travelers went to great pains to avoid flying over or sailing through the area. Although the media emphasized at the time that there is more danger of being killed on the highway than in the Bermuda Triangle, this did little to reassure frightened tourists. Perhaps this is due to the fact that we are not talking of dying but of disappearing. No bodies ever are found after the disappearances in the Devil's Sea – or the Bermuda Triangle – so there always remains the question of what really happened to the people aboard those craft.

Some of the "theories" that have been advanced to explain these disappearances are farfetched: abduction by spacemen; the departure, en masse, of spacemen; a giant "toilet bowl" flush! The more outlandish the theories become the more difficult it is for serious researchers to investigate without being ridiculed. Regardless, scientists and researchers have continued their studies and a number of serious theories have been expounded.

Vincent Gaddis, whose research on the Bermuda Triangle and the Devil's Sea is a cornerstone in the field, wrote in his *Invisible Horizons*, "my own opinion is that within and near the triangle (perhaps, also, in the Devil's Sea and more rarely elsewhere) occasional aberrations of an unusual type occur in the air and on the surface of the ocean. These aberrations might cause magnetic, possibly gravitational, effects, in which case they might for all practical purposes be referred to as 'space-warps,' and cause deadly turbulence ending in total disintegration of planes and ships, for the latter are by no means immune."

Freak storms, waterspouts and undersea volcanoes have been cited as likely causes, but in all these disappearances no evidence of atmospheric or oceanic disturbance was recorded. In any case, as John Godwin states in *This Baffling World*, "Waves cannot be blamed for missing airplanes. And with aircraft, too, we find that almost monotonously fine weather conditions prevailed at the crucial times."

The similarity between the two areas, the Bermuda Triangle and the Devil's Sea, in regard to vanishing ships and planes, is obvious, but the parallels don't end there.

Richard Winer's study, *The Devil's Triangle*, cites the similarity between the magnetic variances in the two areas. It is known that there are compass variations of as much as 20 degrees in various parts of the world. However, Winer points out that "both the western extremity of the 'Devil's Triangle' (he means the Bermuda Triangle) and the western extremity of the 'Devil's Sea' are the only two meridians where the compass actually points to true north." This raises the question of whether some form of magnetic interference is responsible for the phenomena.

The United States Navy conducted a five-year study called Project Magnet in 1945 soon after five aircraft disappeared over the Bermuda Triangle. Many flyers, including entertainer-aviator Arthur Godfrey, testified that while flying through or near these "death sea" areas strange magnetic interference was recorded on navigational instruments. But investigation into this possibility has been inconclusive.

Researchers also are faced with another question: Are there still other "triangles"?

It should be mentioned here that the use of the term "triangle," while convenient, is not technically correct. None of these areas is strictly a triangle, but rather blob- or lozenge-shaped. However, ever since Vincent Gaddis coined the phrase "Bermuda Triangle" this geometric description has stuck.

Whatever their shape, there is growing evidence that there are more than just two of these "triangles." In his *Invisible Residents* Ivan Sanderson writes that continued research brought to light yet another area where there have been similar disappearances, although fewer in number. This area, in the Mediterranean Sea, has claimed several Israeli and French submarines. When he plotted the three areas Sanderson discovered that all three areas lie between 30 degrees and 40 degrees north and spread about 30 degrees east to west. He went on to postulate that three other such areas could exist in the southern hemisphere, and that he found them off the east coasts of South America, South Africa and Australia.

Research may eventually find the solution to the puzzle of these tragic disappearances. But now there are far more questions than there are answers. For scientists the answers may open the doors to new knowledge, but for the pilots and seamen who navigate the "triangles" these answers may be the difference between life and...?

FATE July 1975

THE PHILADELPHIA
EXPERIMENT

I Survived a Journey Through Time

Drue

The Philadelphia Experiment, an alleged World War II attempt to make ships invisible to attackers, is a controversial topic among time travel buffs. Here one author describes what he claims are his long-buried memories of the event.

Under a cloak of darkness on August 15, 1943, those of us aboard the USS *Eldridge* started moving down the Delaware River. As we headed out to sea, we heard and felt an unusual humming sound coming from four powerful generators – a vibration that grew increasingly stronger as we traveled. We felt a sense of apprehension, and routine work came to a halt. Our hair stood on end. An uncommon electrical sensation flowed about the ship. Some men began to shake with fear. The 176 sailors aboard had been trained only in the operation of a naval ship, yet we were about to embark on a secret scientific experiment that had never been attempted before – and that is still underway.

The experiment is known as the Philadelphia Experiment – a mission so secret that even to this day the United States government denies its existence.

The mission had been under development with Dr. Nikola Tesla's guidance since the early 1930s. I got involved in 1938, during the theorem stage, and worked closely with Tesla. My role included preparing and installing equipment on the ship.

Hidden agendas

Shortly after starting work with the project, I was able to distinguish the motives of the groups involved. The three key agendas that were part of this experiment were:

- A scientific agenda to explore the time/space continuum;

- A military agenda. We were fighting World War II, and the military wanted to use invisibility as a weapon, to move personnel and cargo instantaneously;

- An extraterrestrial agenda. Extraterrestrials, working with government officials, wanted to map the Earth's magnetic gridwork for interdimensional travel.

A fourth, closely guarded core agenda also grew among those who worked behind the scenes. Their hidden agenda was to rewrite history. I am not talking about those who are responsible for rewriting our text books, although this has been done. I am discussing physical movement through linear time to change catalogued events in our past and subsequently change the future. Think about the immense power one could have by moving instantly from one event in time to another. Power is what motivated those behind the scenes to conduct the Philadelphia Experiment.

The scientific premise

In 1942, Tesla was given blueprints of a naval warship which he was to equip for the experiment. He was told to include humans – the ship's

The USS Eldridge

crew – in his testing. Tesla knew, however, that the technology had not been perfected. He recognized the dangers that lurked for anyone who would attempt to enter such a tremendous magnetic field.

Tesla made a desperate, passionate attempt to dissuade both the military and the scientists involved in the project from experimenting with humans. To his dismay, he was overwhelmingly overruled. All believed that Tesla's concerns were unfounded and exaggerated. His safety requirements were extensive, expensive, and time-consuming, and with the war effort heating up, military funding was going to be cut if they didn't test the project soon.

Tesla, discouraged, got himself excused by demonstrating instability. History reports that he died in 1943.

After Tesla's departure, during the month of February 1943 the keel of the USS *Eldridge* was laid. While the ship was under construction, we installed technology based upon Tesla's blueprints.

We used four massive generator banks and modified Tesla coils to convert direct current electricity to an alternating current and to step up the frequencies.

As the steady current of electricity was harmonically increased with the help of a prototype of the UNIVAC computer, an awesome magnetic field would encompass the ship. (We did not use jolts or a pulsating current, as some have reported.)

Because Tesla's plans were so extensive, we were directed to take shortcuts. For example, instead of laying all the cable deep within the hull of the ship, we casually laid cables along the outer walls.

The *Eldridge* was launched on July 25, 1943, then sent to the Philadelphia Naval Shipyard for final preparations.

The experiment begins

On August 15, the *Eldridge* made its way out to sea. The experiment did not take place in the Philadelphia harbor or naval shipyard, as people have been led to believe. It took place in the Atlantic Ocean.

Just before dawn, we turned the generators on full strength. None of us was prepared for what was to come.

When we switched the generators to full power, a strong electromagnetic field engulfed the ship. I sensed myself being shaken violently. At the same time, I noted the ship disappearing around me. As if in slow motion, I felt the field propel my entire body outward into hundreds of fragmented pieces. There was a brilliant flash of light and a piercing sound that forced me to the ship's deck. I covered my ears with my hands in a desperate attempt to relieve the pain that wracked my body. Bleeding from my mouth, nose, and ears, I could only wish for death.

Eventually, the chaos around me subsided. I was disoriented. Time, as I knew it, had ceased to exist. I felt stuck in place, unable to move, trapped in an energy field of total darkness. I began to realize that something had gone drastically wrong – just as Tesla had foreseen.

I had to use my entire will and physical strength to break loose from the field of energy that encased me. I moved about the ship taking note of many others who also were in the same predicament. Some were moving about in panic, some were consumed with fire, and others seemed to glow. Some men had been electrocuted because they failed to stay clear of the cables that were laid along the ship's outer walls.

I had to reach the pilot room to locate the captain of the ship in order to assess damages, but he, too, was paralyzed by the powerful force field that had enveloped the ship. I knew we needed to shut down the generators to unplug the operation. The entire ship was transparent, like a dark, red-colored gelatin. Not only could I see through the walls of the ship but move through them as well. Out of desperation, I reached through the wall for one of the generator switches – but it had no substance.

What happened?

Those of us on board were unable to deal with the shocking physical trauma that overwhelmed us. We were paralyzed by fear and a powerful energy field, so the ship's transformers went unchecked.

The chemical makeup of the salty sea water further amplified the transformers' power. The *Eldridge* became a gigantic battery, emitting forces beyond imagination. The amount of energy used for the experiment was obviously overkill, like using 2,000 sticks of dynamite for a one-stick job. We created a 1,540-ton magnet using in excess of 150 billion volts!

Once we connected with the earth's magnetic grid, its pulsating nature clutched us in its grasp; the pulsating current that so many have talked about came from the grid, not the technology. Unanticipated, the magnetic field that we created not only caused electrical disturbances with the grid itself, but a mind-boggling paradox.

Traveling through time

Before we knew what was happening, the ship and its crew were fragmented into different dimensions and magnetically pulled through time and space. The experiment had been designed to move the *Eldridge* from one location to another; unexpectedly, we also moved through time.

The initial surge shot us from our position in the Atlantic on August 15, 1943, to Niagara Falls in approximately 3543.

During the experiment, two of the ship's generator banks were consumed by fire, and the specialized electron tubes exploded randomly because of electrical overload. With this loss of power, we started to decompress, bouncing around the grid like a rock skipping across a pond. We were unstable and totally out of control.

To those of us on board, time ceased to exist. To some, our movement from place to place seemed to take hours. In some cases, the movement seemed to occur instantly. And at times, our existence on the ship seemed to last for an eternity. In fact, our concept of time was radically altered.

A magnetic attraction

The *Eldridge* traveled from place to place, pulled by magnetic forces across the globe. It's interesting to note that all of the locations we visited experienced strong electromagnetic storms and electrical blackouts prior to our arrival. We drained each area's source of commercial power, causing major blackouts. If you closely review a map of the United States and compare it to the locations we visited, you will see that the majority of the sites have a major water basin created by artificial dams. It was the massive generators operating at these locations and the magnetic fields they created that pulled us through time and space.

We traveled to a number of locations, including the Norfolk Naval Base in 1944, the Armistad Reservoir in 1954 Texas, Arizona's Lake Powell in 1966, Chicago in 1969, New Mexico's Navajo Reservoir in 1977, and Nevada's Lake Mead in 1983.

Some of the sites we visited are still in our present-day future. I have approximated dates and geographical locations, since I am still conducting my research. I have determined, however, that the *Eldridge* will again materialize as early as this year [1997], either on the Colorado River or on Maine's Sebago Lake. Future appearances include California's Imperial Reservoir in 2005 and Utah's Great Salt Lake in 2043.

Many people are familiar with previous accounts of our movement to the Naval Base located in Norfolk, Virginia. This movement was not caused by dam generators, but by generators on naval ships. These ships, known as floating power stations, provide ship-to-shore electrical power when no other means is available.

Help from the military

In 1977, the *Eldridge* materialized long enough at the Navajo Reservoir in New Mexico to make contact with military authorities. We were counting on a window of at least 72 hours to reassess our situation before we would be pulled once again through time.

In addition to the two burnt generators, our AT&T radio equipment also had been damaged as we moved. We had to make do with our remaining communications equipment – so some of us disembarked to set up an antenna.

The military was not prepared for us when we made contact, but after confirming our position, they secured the area. Many of the *Eldridge*'s men were wounded and badly in need of medical attention. Thirty-three of the sickest men were taken off the ship and taken to military research laboratories. Military officials gave us additional medical supplies and replacement parts for some of the damaged equipment. However, much of what we needed was still not aboard when the window closed.

After we were pulled away from the New Mexico site, there was a massive effort by the scientific and military communities to end the ordeal for those of us on board.

Six years later, in 1983, the scientific community finally understood what it would take to stabilize our energy field. They now knew the crucial ingredients required to put the brakes on our movement. Importantly, one was fresh water. Experimenting near Las Vegas, Nevada, scientists induced our frequencies in order to pull us to Lake Mead. Once the ship was stabilized, we were able to rematerialize. Again, damaged equipment – including the burned-out generators – was replaced.

At the same time, another 87 men were taken off the *Eldridge* for research purposes. Without exception, they had been exposed to extreme levels of radiation, and their days were numbered.

In 1983, military authorities at Lake Mead selected 19 men to board the *Eldridge* and assist us back home. The men went back in time with us to August 16, 1943. Their mission: damage control and cleanup. We were successfully teleported back through time to our original point of departure. We arrived during the daylight hours of Monday, August 16, 1943.

The mission of the 19 men with us, whom I refer to as the cleanup crew, was multi-purposed. One was a presidential observer from the Reagan administration who met with members of the Roosevelt Administration, three were hazardous waste experts, two were medical professionals, one was a military historian, four were "timeliners," and the rest were scientists. When they completed their missions, 15 members of the cleanup crew boarded the *Eldridge* on August 18, 1943 and returned to 1983. However, instead of returning to the Lake Mead site from which they originated, they returned to Montauk Point, Long Island, New York, where other research into time and space is reportedly underway. The remaining four crew members, the timeliners, stayed in 1943.

As soon as our ship arrived back in 1943, we made radio communications with the observation vessel. Because our return was some 24 hours after the experiment had begun, those aboard the observation vessel were frantic – and they were completely unprepared for what they were about to encounter.

The *Eldridge* was nothing more than a molten piece of twisted iron. She was extremely radioactive and unquestionably unstable. Struck by the physical condition of the ship and of those of us on board, those who had been waiting for our return swiftly radioed for urgent medical assistance.

We were taken off the ship and placed under medical sequester on board a US Navy medical ship. I remember looking back at the horrific, still-smoldering *Eldridge*. As the sun shone brightly, naval personnel were frantically trying to get things under control. Many of the men and women that were part of the rescue mission were overwhelmed by the stench of the burning and decomposing flesh left behind. Some from the other ships even refused to board the *Eldridge*.

Of the 181 men aboard, only 21 survived. Forty men were confirmed dead as a result of radiation exposure, burns, electrocution and fright. Twenty-seven of these 40 men were embedded within the structure of the ship, but they were not all dead. Mercifully, some were shot in the head using a standard military pistol – yet others were kept alive long enough for laboratory research. The other 120 men were never accounted for. These were the men removed from the ship on our Nevada and New Mexico stops, but to observers in 1943, they had simply disappeared.

The lost survivors

Uncertain of the radiation levels that had bombarded the observation and medical ships' crews, military officials also placed observers in medical confinement.

The Naval Department was faced with the grim task of having to inform family members of their loved ones' demise aboard the *Eldridge*. The explanation they gave? Missing in action. The Navy had to handle civilian cases differently. My family was told that I had come into contact with a deadly strain of meningitis and that I had died in a quarantined government institution. Both explanations were perfect cover-ups.

Naval authorities in 1943 were faced with a second dilemma: how to explain the disappearance of an entire ship and her crew and at the same time keep the experiment secret.

Authorities had major hurdles to overcome: The *Eldridge* had been secretly launched, and the experiment took place on August 15, 1943 – prior to her official commissioning on August 27. Officials could not use the war to explain her loss. So, they simply came up with a replacement ship.

They chose to substitute a prototype destroyer escort for the *Eldridge*. Prototypes are not normally placed within the military's operating inventories, so they don't come under the same stringent rules of accounting. As a result, the Navy took advantage of their immediate access to a ship that closely resembled the *Eldridge* used in the experiment.

When World War II concluded, the decoy was decommissioned and taken out of service. Approximately six years later, in 1951, the surrogate *Eldridge* was transferred to the country of Greece under the Mutual Defense Assistance program. Now known as the *Lion*, the ship is still in service.

A lost life

Those of us who survived the experiment were never to see our family, friends or the outside world again. The military kept the 21 of us confined, sedated and under close medical observation. We became laboratory research material, in the process losing everything we had, including our most precious belonging – our individuality. Debriefings took place directly after our return, and it was from these proceedings that I knew this was just the beginning of a cover-up.

For reasons of secrecy, the military kept all of us out at sea on a small medical ship for some time. When other arrangements could be made, we were moved to different locations on land throughout the United States. I was bandaged from head to toe and moved to Northern California as a burn victim. In 1944, after agreeing to participate in another time-related experiment, I was moved to Nevada.

Because my physical body was dying as a result of radiation exposure, government scientists offered me a chance to take part in a second experiment, known as the ET Program, which was short for electronic transmigration. Using electricity, my spirit, my personality, was sent forward through time to approximately the year 1962, and I was moved into the body of a young boy who – unbeknownst to his family – was about to die. In the process, scientists also erased my memory of my personal history and of the Philadelphia Experiment. I simply assumed the boy's place in his family, without any knowledge of my true identity. While my physical body is now 44, memories of my real age and my true history began to resurface just a few years ago.

241

I am still researching the events surrounding the Philadelphia Experiment, and trying to reconstruct my life. If anything, however, the Philadelphia Experiment has taught me the true essence of time: It is not linear – past, present, and future – but parallel. Time is only an event, with all events happening simultaneously now.

Drue retired from the US Marine Corps in 1993 after 22 years. Just prior to his retirement, he started to experience flashbacks of the Philadelphia Experiment. He started investigating the story. Drue uses just one name, because that's how he is known to other Eldridge survivors.

FATE February 1997

THE PHILADELPHIA EXPERIMENT: ON THE TRAIL OF A TIME TRAVELER

Janet Brennan

Since I was a child I've been fascinated by the supernatural, and I've often wondered what it would be like to be a paranormal investigator. Thanks to FATE magazine, I got to find out.

My adventure started in July 1997. I had my first story assignment: Drive up to Sebago Lake, Maine, and see if a time-traveling World War II destroyer would appear on August 15 as predicted.

At first, I was sure I'd be wasting my time. I'm not a science fiction fan and physics was never my strong suit, but I'm certain that time travel is impossible now, and it certainly was 50 years ago. But after I read the story of the USS *Eldridge* in the February 1997 issue of FATE, I began to believe that maybe it could have happened.

The story was written by a man known only as Drue. He claims he was a sailor on the *Eldridge* when it was the subject of a government research project called the Philadelphia Experiment, begun in the early

1930s. Drue says the ship was fitted with four massive generator banks and modified Tesla coils. The government intended to teleport the ship from one location to another. But when scientists fired up the generators at dawn on August 15, 1943, the electromagnetic field they created was more powerful than they had expected. The ship began moving, not only through space but through time as well – from the Atlantic Ocean to Niagara Falls thousands of years in the future – to 3543.

Drue claims that the ship jumped to at least 10 different locations and times in the United States, including seven locations between 1943 and 1997. The hellish experience was more like a horror movie than a sci-fi flick. The generators caught fire and exploded. The ship and its crew were exposed to radiation, from which some sailors died. Others were electrocuted. Most grotesquely, 27 men were embedded in the structure of the ship as their molecules fragmented.

The hideous ordeal lasted about 24 hours in linear time, says Drue. During the ship's appearances in the future, government officials boarded to repair the generators and move the sickest men off the boat, where they apparently remained living in what was, to them, the future. Of the original crew of 181, only 21 (including Drue) made it back alive to their point of departure, arriving during the day on August 16, 1943.

Drue claims that during the experiment, the ship materialized on either the Colorado River or Sebago Lake on August 15, 1997. So here I was, traveling to Sebago to see if the Navy vessel would really show up.

On the morning of August 15, I set out to see if I could capture a warship – on film. I drafted my husband as chauffeur; my teenage son, a longtime *Dr. Who* fan, rode shotgun as my resident time-travel consultant.

As we made the drive from our home to the lake, the beautiful weather was an ominous sign. Drue had written that the ship was pulled from place to place by the Earth's magnetic forces, and that all the locations it visited experienced strong electromagnetic storms and power blackouts just prior to the ship's arrival. But as we approached Sebago Lake, the sun shone in a sapphire sky and only a gentle breeze stirred the crisp air. The bright day was dimming my hopes of seeing anything happen out on the clear, blue waters of the 12-mile-long lake.

The lake covers 47 square miles, is eight miles wide at its widest point, and has a maximum depth of 316 feet – big enough to hold a Navy destroyer.

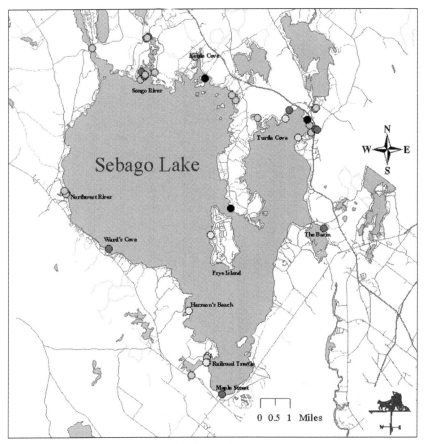

Map of Sebago Lake, Maine

I asked a local fisherman who was taking his boat out of the water if he'd seen anything on the water that morning. Nope, he replied, all was quiet.

Drue claims that most of the sites the *Eldridge* visited have a major water basin created by artificial dams. "It was the massive generators operating at these locations and the magnetic fields they created that pulled us through time and space," he wrote.

Sebago Lake was formed by glaciers thousands of years ago and has no hydroelectric dams on it. But the water company operates an ozone facility on the shore, so I decided to head there and see if I could discover whether that might house any generators that could attract a time-traveling ship.

We drove down the eastern shore of the lake (always keeping an eye out for a destroyer) to the ozone facility and there we hit pay dirt. This building, the largest ozone plant in New England, creates ozone for use as a water disinfectant.

In nature, ozone is produced when lightning splits oxygen molecules in the air. But in the disinfection plant, ozone is created by applying very high voltage power to dielectric tubes containing dried air.

The process requires a high voltage of electricity. James Wallace, the plant's chief operator, told us that power supplied by the local electric utility enters the plant at 460 volts. Then the ozone plant's transformers increase the voltage to 16,000, the amount needed to create ozone. Large electrical generators are also located in the facility so that pumping and water treatment can continue even when the power fails.

I left the ozone facility confident that the two necessary ingredients for the *Eldridge's* appearance were in place – a large, deep body of water and a major power source nearby. We headed back to the shore to watch and wait.

It was 4 PM at the Standish boat ramp, and Laurie Soucik, a vacationer from Barberton, Ohio, was taking her boat out of the lake. She'd been on the water since 10 AM and had seen nothing. Docked nearby was the Portland Water District's lake inspector, Walt Smith. His job is to patrol all 47 square miles of the lake to check for polluters or any other problems that could endanger water quality. He'd been on the lake from 8 AM to 3:30 PM, and he reported nothing more exciting than perfect weather and less boat traffic than he expected to see. He saw no suspicious-looking fog banks and certainly no Navy destroyers. I snapped a few photos of the calm lake, checked it out through my binoculars (nothing), and examined the compass for magnetic fluctuations (none). Then we drove up the western side of the lake.

By this point, late in the afternoon, high, thin clouds were moving in, giving the sky a milky appearance, but the weather was still fair as we ensconced ourselves at Long Beach in the town of East Sebago.

Dinnertime arrived, and we settled on the outdoor deck of the Sebago Wave restaurant, located right on the water at Long Beach. As we ate we could gaze across the widest and deepest part of Sebago, known as

Big Bay. This, I felt, was the most likely part of the lake to spot the ship. But a lone sailboat and a few motorboats were the only craft on the water.

Watching their lazy meanderings and sipping a cold draft beer with my lobster roll were beginning to lull me into a state of somnolent relaxation, when suddenly I spotted large puffs of gray smoke floating over the lake. Could this be from a fire aboard the *Eldridge*? My heart pounding, I leaped up and grabbed the binoculars, mentally berating myself for having already used up almost my whole roll of film.

But through the binoculars I could see that the smoke was not coming from a destroyer or anything else on the lake, but from behind trees at the far northern tip. Later, I found out from news reports that a large house fire in the town of Naples was the source of the smoke.

As evening crept in, I sat on a dock, dangled my feet in the crystal water, and took my last look at Sebago Lake. I was a little disappointed that my big story turned out to be a bust. Then I thought about the death and destruction Drue described on a ship that, out of control in the time-space grid, became "a molten piece of twisted iron." Was I really sorry that it didn't show up in Maine that summer day? Or maybe even that it never really happened?

No, I wasn't sorry. Not at all.

Janet Brennan: FATE contributor, newspaper editor and freelance writer.

FATE November 1997

Proof of the Philadelphia Experiment?

W. Ritchie Benedict

It is the dream of every researcher that at some point he or she will discover dramatic, hidden information about a well-established case. We hear talk of "the smoking gun" or "the silver bullet," and there are many historical cases that could still have unexpected treasures to reveal. Examples might include the thunderbird photograph, Roswell, the mystery ship *Ellen Austin,* and the Loys South American primate photo. With that in mind, I was somewhat hopeful, but rather wary, when I began my current research.

The Philadelphia Experiment has been one of the most controversial events in the realm of the unknown. In the summer of 1943, the US Navy was supposedly engaged in electronic experiments to render ships invisible. It is said that Albert Einstein was one of the scientists directly involved. According to legend, the USS *Eldridge,* a manned destroyer escort, vanished from its berth in Philadelphia, appeared briefly in Norfolk, then teleported itself back to Philadelphia. The experiment apparently had extremely unpleasant side effects for the crew – some were embedded in the bulkhead, some burst into flames, and some vanished from sight never to be seen again. Due to this disaster, any further experimentation was discontinued. A movie was made in 1984 roughly based on the legend.

Any proof that such an experiment was actually attempted is in short supply and rests mainly on the claims of a man named Carlos Allende [aka Carl Meredith Allen], who may have served as a crewman on the ship. Some researchers totally dismiss Allende as an attention-seeking hoaxer. However, one piece of evidence that could substantiate his story has now been located. It is a newspaper clipping, undated and without identification as to origin. William Moore and Charles Berlitz devote substantial space to it in their 1979 book, *The Philadelphia Experiment*. It reads as follows:

Strange Circumstances Surround Tavern Brawl
Several city police officers responding to a call to aid members of the Navy Shore Patrol in breaking up a tavern brawl near the US Navy docks here last night got something of a surprise when they arrived on the scene to find the place empty of customers. According to a pair of very nervous waitresses, the Shore Patrol had arrived first and cleared the place out – but not before two of the sailors involved allegedly did a disappearing act.

"They just sort of vanished into thin air...right there," reported one of the frightened hostesses, "and I ain't been drinking either." At that point, according to her account, the Shore Patrol proceeded to hustle everybody out of the place in short order.

A subsequent chat with the local police precinct left no doubts as to the fact that some sort of general brawl had indeed occurred in the vicinity of the dockyards at about eleven o'clock last night, but neither confirmation nor denial of the stranger aspects of the story could be immediately obtained. One reported witness succinctly summed up the affair by dismissing it as nothing more than "a lot of hooey from them daffy dames down there," who, he went on to say, were probably looking for some free publicity.

Damage to the tavern was estimated to be in the vicinity of six hundred dollars.

Moore and Berlitz considered the possibility that the clipping could have been from a Camden or Newark paper because the column width was greater than any of the Philadelphia dailies of the 1940s. Other sources mentioned have referred to *Life* and *Male* magazines and the *New York Telegram* as having published articles on the subject.

I wish to state right now that I have not located the newspaper clipping in question. But I did find something equally as strange and better documented that might shed some light on the mystery. As I skimmed through pages of Canadian newspapers on the microfilm reader, I reflected that the chances of finding one tiny, obscure item from an eastern US newspaper were next to nonexistent. Several years ago, I heard that no one has been able to uncover the tavern brawl incident because it might have been printed in one of the military base newspapers of the period.

One thing I checked while searching was the death of my paternal grandmother at the young age of 50 in January 1937. I found her obituary in the *Calgary Herald* and then decided to look in some of the other newspapers for the same month, because some of the articles interested me. It was then I discovered the following brief item in the *Edmonton Bulletin* for January 26, 1937:

Italy Savant Discovers Ray for Invisibility *ROME, January 26 – A ray which makes people or things completely invisible has been discovered by an Italian scientist, according to the newspaper* Secolo-Sera.

An experiment is described in which the ray was turned on two women engaged in conversation.

They gradually faded out of sight, until they disappeared completely, but their voices could still be heard in argument.

Not much to go on, to be sure, and as always with these things, more questions are raised than answered. It took a lot more digging. This article did not appear to be in any of the other major newspapers, but I eventually found a mention in a small-town newspaper – *The Carbon Chronicle* of Carbon, Alberta, for January 21, 1937. Headlined "New Electrical Rays," the subtitle states: "Italian Invention Makes Man Invisible By Use of This Apparatus" and continues:

> *Engineer Mario Mancini of Milan was reported ready to offer the world an electro-optical apparatus which makes a man invisible while under its rays. Professor Mancini's machine was described as an electrical device whose levers regulate the intensity and frequency of electrical current in order to obtain its rays. Newspaper reports are that the apparatus, the result of years of work, has been patented. While X-rays render invisible only the softer parts of the body, the Mancini rays are reported to penetrate every part. It is asserted that in tests at the professor's home persons subjected to the rays were invisible, while the chairs in which they sat could be seen. Few substances, it was added, are able to stop the rays.*
>
> *Informants asserted that persons subjected to the rays first assume a confused appearance, then become ghost-like, and finally become invisible.*

What are we to make of this? Who was Mario Mancini, and did he do what he said he did – a full six years before the Philadelphia Experiment? It certainly offers a number of new avenues for research – the name of a major Italian newspaper, the *Secolo Sera*; exact dates; the location (Milan) of the experiment; and the name of the scientist as well. However, due to limited resources, I have been unable to find out any more along this line.

We must consider the possibility that the whole thing was a hoax or a propaganda exercise by the Italian government boasting about its scientific achievements. But why does it bear such remarkable similarities to the purported side effects of the US experiment? Then, too, a patent is mentioned. Unless every trace was destroyed in the Allied bombing raids of World War II, it should be possible to locate some other sources of information about the Mancini experiment.

If this report is authentic, the mystery is why Mussolini's secret police didn't latch on to it immediately. In the August 2000 issue of FATE, columnist J. Antonio Huneeus dealt extensively with some files that have recently come to light on UFO activity in Italy in the 1930s. There is some doubt as to their authenticity, but they appear genuine based on the color of the paper and ink aging tests. A mysterious department known as "Cabinet RS/33" was charged with investigating UFO reports, and when World War II began, the Cabinet's secrets were shared with, and literally shipped to, Nazi Germany. Did any of these shipments include the Mancini experiments? Did Mancini destroy his own work, lest it fall into the hands of the Nazis? Or was he secretly transported to the US to take up work on American experiments into invisibility? Perhaps the Italian government ignored him completely, believing him to be just another crackpot inventor? Or were the results shelved as being too dangerous and erratic? There were a number of now forgotten inventors in the 1930s working on experiments dealing with free energy and death rays, but most if not all of these were before their time and were impractical. The Mancini experiments could have fallen into this category and been totally forgotten.

Another remarkable discovery I made relates to invisibility and concerns two classic cases of Forteana. The infamous David Lang disappearance case has been discredited as an example of an urban legend cooked up by a 19th-century newspaperman. The story goes that on the afternoon of September 23, 1880, Daniel Lang of Sumner County, Tennessee, crossed a field in full view of his wife and two children as a judge and his brother-in-law approached in a buggy. He suddenly vanished from sight forever, and an irregular circle 15 feet in diameter marked his departure point. His children heard his voice calling from the circle months later. It has been suggested that the tale came from author Ambrose Bierce, who managed his own mysterious disappearance in Mexico in 1913.

Another version of the tale says it happened in 1854 in Selma, Alabama, to a planter named Williamson. Equally annoying is the account of Charles Ashmore/Oliver Lerch/Oliver Larch/Oliver Thomas, who went to the well on a farm in South Bend, Indiana/Wales in

1878/1890/1909, leaving footprints that abruptly stopped in the snow. FATE writer Joe Nickell checked the Indiana archives to no avail. Again, Ambrose Bierce was to blame, as he published a story about Ashmore in 1893 that was set in Quincy, Illinois, in November 1878.

I had long ago written off these tales when I came across something startling in the *Regina Leader Post* for October 10, 1901. A newspaper account of mysterious disappearances mentions both cases and for the first time gives specific locations – locations, moreover, that are not in the United States. The relevant passage begins halfway down the column and states:

A typical example of this [mysterious vanishings] occurred some forty years ago, near the village of Haslemere, in Surrey, England. One morning a respectable farmer named Williamson started to cross a big meadow near his home, for the purpose of giving instructions to a man who was working on the other side. He trudged along, whistling and singing, to the middle of the field and there suddenly and unaccountably vanished. There was no wall, no ditch, no bush even, which could have concealed the missing man for a moment. His wife, who was standing at the door with her baby in her arms watching him, screamed out, 'He's gone! He's gone! What an awful thing!' and fell to the ground unconscious. When she revived, her reason had fled and two other women, who witnessed the strange occurrence, received so severe a fright that they were unable to pursue their accustomed vocations for many weeks afterwards. No light was ever thrown upon this mystery, and to this day, the strangest stories are afloat in the district concerning it.

Likewise, a paragraph is devoted to Ashmore, starting:

From a house situated on the main road between Steyning and Bramber, about nine o'clock in the evening, a lad of thirteen named Charles Ashmore was sent with a bucket to a well 100 yards or so distant to procure water. When he did not return, the family became anxious and his father set out with a lantern to seek him. A light coating of snow covered the ground, though none was falling, or had fallen for some hours, and the footsteps of the boy were distinctly traced to a spot about halfway between the house and the well. At this point, they suddenly ceased, nothing but the unbroken surface of the snow being visible in front and all around.

For the first time, we have an English setting for both stories, even though the dates are somewhat vague. With Williamson, it has to be somewhere between 1854 and 1861, and Ashmore could be anywhere from the 1860s to the late 1870s. A little known fact is that Ambrose Bierce paid a visit to Britain in about 1872-74. My theory is that he heard both of these stories, which were then fairly recent, and Americanized them for his reading public. After that, confusion set in, and it has been utterly impossible to discover their original source – until now.

Being a writer, Bierce would naturally have a nose for a good tale. He may have had his reasons for changing names or locations – the threat of a lawsuit. Another newspaper article from Newfoundland in 1910 elicited the further information that Mrs. Williamson was confined to an asylum. If her relatives were alive when Bierce visited England, as they could well have been, the writer could have found himself the unwanted recipient of a major lawsuit. Mental illness in those days was regarded as a major disgrace. He probably altered the names, and by the 1930s the story had become hopelessly muddled. (The December 28, 1938, edition of the *Halifax Herald*, for example, ran a lengthy piece giving the familiar background of "Thomas Lerch" in South Bend, Indiana.)

It should be possible for the first time, given the geographic location, to search the papers of the approximate dates for more details. I have attempted to chew my way through the *Manchester Guardian* for the late 1850s, but unfortunately, it and the *London Times* are the only papers to which I have access on microfilm.

Why is the proof of the Philadelphia Experiment, or the Mancini experimentation, or the Williamson/Ashmore cases of any importance to us today? After all, they happened many decades ago, or even a century or more in the past. They are significant today because any form of confirmation could lead to the greatest leap in science in human history – something totally mind-boggling, directly out of science-fiction. It has long been speculated that other dimensions exist adjacent to our own, separated by their unique electromagnetic signatures. Suppose we could place an object (or a person) in a powerful rotating field sufficiently strong to cause all the constituent electrons to shift orbits simultaneously (a quantum leap?). Then that object, or person, might end up somewhere! Somewhere that definitely is not "here." You would not have to travel through a black hole and be crushed out of existence in order to enter another reality. The vacuum-tube technology of the 1930s and 1940s would not really be capable of sustaining an effort of this nature, but we would certainly be able to do so today, particularly with computers to control the fields generated by supercooled magnets. In 1946, the first computer, Univac, used vacuum tubes that were always having to be replaced. Is this the factor that doomed the Philadelphia Experiment and possibly the Mancini experimentation to failure?

The Williamson/Ashmore cases are important because we must also consider the possibility that powerful electromagnetic vortices exist naturally and periodically within the earth's own electromagnetic field. These could be strong enough to transport any hapless human or animal caught in them to an alternate reality. The only way of returning would be to enter the vortex on the other side at the exact right moment and time, something poor Williamson and Ashmore would not be capable of doing without a lot more knowledge. If the *Eldridge* teleported instead of vanishing entirely, it could mean that it popped up in the nearest available vortex node, which happened to be in Norfolk, Virginia, rather than managing the transition to another reality. It is possible that the ancients knew about these vortices all along and chose to mark the spots with pyramids, henges and other megalithic forms of architecture.

The implications are far beyond the scope of this article, but we could potentially have invisibility, teleportation, transfer to an alternate universe and maybe even time travel as well. It might be necessary for subjects to wear a special suit and helmet to avoid any physical consequences of exposure to these forces.

A thought just struck me – a machine generating a powerful rotating electromagnetic field, that can appear and disappear into another dimension at will, with occupants that wear special suits. Oh, yes. I think they call them UFOs.

[Carlos Allende died on March 5, 1994 at the age of 68. His story is widely regarded as a hoax.]

W. Ritchie Benedict (1943-2011): Canadian writer, researcher and lecturer on Fortean phenomena and UFOs; a frequent contributor to FATE.

FATE April 2001

About FATE Magazine

Six decades before reality TV shows and late-night radio's *Coast to Coast AM*, and countless websites, blogs, books, and movies began captivating audiences with true tales of Ufos and the paranormal – there was FATE – a first-of-its-kind publication dedicated to in-depth coverage of mysterious and unexplained phenomena.

FATE was a true journalistic pioneer, covering issues like electronic voice phenomena, cattle mutilations, life on Mars, telepathic communication with animals, and UFOs at a time when discussing such things was neither hip nor trendy. Today FATE enjoys a rare longevity achieved by only a select few US periodicals.

Where it all began: The birth of the modern UFO era

The year was 1948. The Cold War was in its infancy, and the Space Age was still a dream...but across the nation and around the world, people observed strange objects flying through the skies.

Two Chicago-based magazine editors, Raymond A. Palmer and Curtis B. Fuller, took a close look at the public's fascination with flying saucers and saw the opportunity of a lifetime. With help from connections in the worlds of science fiction and alternative spirituality, they launched a new magazine dedicated to the objective exploration of the world's mysteries. They gave their "cosmic reporter" the name FATE.

FATE's first issue, published in Spring 1948, featured as its cover story the firsthand report of pilot Kenneth Arnold on his UFO sighting of the previous year, an event widely recognized by UFO historians as the birth of the modern UFO era.

FATE's role in creating a new genre: The paranormal

Other topics covered in this and subsequent issues included vanished civilizations, communication with spirits, synchronicity, exotic religions, monsters and giants, out-of-place artifacts, and phenomena too bizarre for categorization. This mix of subjects set a template that the magazine would follow for six decades and counting. In many ways, FATE magazine created the genre that is now known as "the paranormal."

Palmer and Fuller's judgment of FATE's potential proved correct, and as demand for the magazine grew its publication frequency increased quickly from quarterly to bimonthly to monthly. Palmer sold his share of the magazine in the late 1950s, and Fuller brought his wife, Mary, aboard to help run the growing business.

FATE's success spawned scores of imitators over the years, but none lasted very long. Through the decades FATE kept going, doggedly promoting the validity of paranormal studies but unafraid to reveal major events as hoaxes or frauds when it was warranted. Among the famous cases debunked by FATE were the Philadelphia Experiment, and the book and movie versions of the Amityville Horror.

Relevant today

So how does FATE still stay relevant after all this time? Especially in a fast-paced, high-tech world that is often short on attention span and long on cynicism, how does a magazine like FATE continue to thrive? Editor-in-Chief Phyllis Galde says, "FATE allows readers to think for themselves by providing them with stories that mainstream publications don't dare touch. The truth is, reality does not conform to the neat and tidy box that many people would like to wedge it into. Our world is a bizarre and wondrous place and our universe is filled with mystery – it is teeming with the unknown. People are longing for something more than the mundane transactions of everyday existence. FATE feeds the soul's appetite for the enigmatic, the esoteric, and the extraordinary."

Subscribe to FATE

FATE is published in intervals throughout the year in a popular digest size. Join the family of subscribers by visiting the FATE website at www.fatemag.com.

ABOUT ROSEMARY ELLEN GUILEY

Rosemary Ellen Guiley, executive editor of *FATE* magazine, is a leading expert in the metaphysical and paranormal fields, with more than 65 books published on a wide range of paranormal, UFO, cryptid, spiritual and mystical topics, including nine single-volume encyclopedias and reference works. Her work focuses on interdimensional entity contact experiences of all kinds (spirit, alien, creature), the afterlife and spirit communications, problem hauntings, spirit and entity attachments, psychic skills, dreamwork for well-being, spiritual growth and development, angels, past and parallel lives, and investigation of unusual paranormal activity. She has worked full-time as an investigator, researcher, author, and presenter since 1983, and spends a great deal of time in the field doing original research.

Rosemary is president and owner of Visionary Living, Inc., a publishing and media company. She makes numerous appearances on radio and in documentaries, docudramas and television shows.

A personal note from Rosemary

I have been privileged to be part of the FATE family since 1991-92. Dennis Stillings, the publisher of *Artifex* magazine, brought me to the Minneapolis area to give a lecture on vampires – my book *Vampires Among Us* had just been published. In the audience were Phyllis Galde and David Godwin, editors of FATE. They invited me to contribute to FATE, and a lasting friendship was struck.

I started as a columnist for FATE; my column was called "Gateways." I joined the prestigious company of other FATE columnists and regulars, among them John A. Keel, Mark Chorvinsky, Loyd Auerbach, Antonio Huneeus, and Loren Coleman.

Over the course of time, FATE went through changes. Phyllis and David departed to set up their own publishing company, Galde Press. In the early 2000s, they purchased FATE from Llewellyn. David passed in 2012, and FATE remains under Phyllis's ownership. The economic upheavals in publishing, combined with rapid changes in the delivery of information, have impacted FATE. One a monthly magazine, it is now published several times a year – still delivering the same varied and insightful content.

I went from columnist to consulting editor, and in 2016 became Executive Editor, taking on more editing responsibilities. Phyllis and I entered into a partnership to bring you a series of books on the best from the archives of FATE on timeless topics of ongoing interest. FATE has thousands of excellent articles in its vaults, written by the best of the best, and I am pleased to make them available again.

Printed in Great Britain
by Amazon

75913247R00166